FAMILY STYLE CHINESE COOKBOOK
中国老百姓的家常菜谱

FAMILY STYLE
CHINESE
COOKBOOK

Authentic Recipes from
My Culinary Journey Through China

SHANTI CHRISTENSEN

Foreword by Bee Yin Low
Photography by Nadine Greeff

ROCKRIDGE
PRESS

For the families who welcomed me into their homes and taught me how to cook Chinese food. And to my loving and supportive husband Paul and our son Miles, a budding foodie.

CONTENTS

FOREWORD

I am humbled and honored to introduce Shanti Christensen's debut cookbook *Family Style Chinese Cookbook*, partly because I feel like I shared in her adventure. In 2006, I had recently started a blog about Asian cuisine called *Rasa Malaysia*. I was traveling to Beijing extensively when I met Shanti through my colleague, Peikwen Cheng. We had a lot in common, including a love for food, travel, and great laughs. Over the course of many scrumptious and mouthwatering Chinese meals, we became friends. We often shared many of our culinary dreams and aspirations.

Shanti started her blog *ShowShanti* in 2009 and I loved it from the start. It's gorgeous, colorful, and engaging and shares her personal journey of learning about authentic Chinese cooking. From my computer screen I followed Shanti religiously as she trekked through rural China. She had little fear, huge passion, and an immense appetite to learn about Chinese cuisine. Her

assistant-cum-translator, Juling He, traveled with her into the private homes of her hosts, where they would tell Shanti stories and teach her home-style Chinese cooking. With the knowledge and techniques she learned, she honed her own Chinese cooking skills in her kitchen.

Family Style Chinese Cookbook is a treasure trove of real Chinese home cooking. But it's more than just a cookbook. It's a collection of stories about tradition, ceremony, family, and pride. Within these pages are adventures for anyone who wishes to feel themselves transported—perhaps to a warm and tiny kitchen in Tongzhou for a communal meal with dear friends, or to a potholed alleyway packed with the sights and smells of food vendors' delights. I have no doubt that I will relive the wonderful tastes, smells, aromas, and memories of China through this book. *Ganbei!*

BEE YINN LOW
Author of *Easy Chinese Recipes*

INTRODUCTION

With more people than all of North America and Europe combined, the People's Republic of China occupies a broad swath of territory. Whether from a geographic, cultural, historical, religious, political, economic, or even linguistic perspective, the country's people and places vary as much as those of entire continents. And its food is no different. Chinese cuisine is a colorful adventure that draws explorers into a long history rich with stories, traditions, and influences. I am one of those explorers.

My love for food and travel started with my parents. My Danish-American father is an avid reader and a Korean War veteran. He enjoyed traveling and discovered an affinity for Eastern culture. He had moved to Guam to work as a carpenter and met my mother's father, who is from the Philippines. One day, my "Lolo" (grandpa in Tagalog) showed my dad a photo of his daughter and asked if he might like to write to her. They began

Opposite, clockwise: Noodles served in an alleyway in Pingyao, an ancient city in Shanxi province. Ingredients prepped before a lesson in cooking home-style Chinese cuisine. The author doing what she loves most, exploring markets and discovering new ingredients.

exchanging letters, talking about politics, and my dad appreciated my mom's distaste for the then dictator Ferdinand Marcos. He sent for her to meet him in Guam, but martial law was imposed and she was unable to leave the Philippines. So my dad hopped on a plane to the Philippines, where he met the entire family and soon married her.

From there, my parents moved to Guam and traveled to India and Southeast Asia, and even lived in Japan for a year to teach English. They spent five years traveling Asia before returning to Guam to start a family. Eventually they moved to California. I spent many happy hours as a child listening to stories about their travels and the foods they had enjoyed. My mother introduced me to a wide range of foods. She cooked a variety of cuisines from her Filipino heritage, which blends cooking influences from Spain, China, and other cultures in the Southeast Pacific.

My first chance to travel was as a student ambassador for Stockton's sister city in Japan, Shimizu, a scenic port that overlooks Mount Fuji. I traveled again after college, that time solo, through the Far East to Nepal,

India, Thailand, Vietnam, Cambodia, Taipei, and finally to Hong Kong and Shanghai. Even after five months of travel, I still felt the pull of the explorer within me.

In 2007, I was engaged to Peikwen Cheng, someone as adventurous as I was and, who shared my desire to live in China in the year leading up to the 2008 Beijing Olympics. We left our home in San Francisco and moved to Shanghai with two suitcases each. He found a job working with MySpace China and I initially worked as a freelance graphic designer and later as a food editor for *Time Out Beijing*.

We arrived on a cold, drizzly night, dropped off our luggage at our apartment, and walked to Lost Heaven restaurant for our first of many nights out to come in Shanghai. During the next six years, we would get married in Beijing (and later divorced), and our lives followed a hectic yet invigorating pace.

In Shanghai, I spent months trying to learn Mandarin while feeling a new sense of self being sculpted each day. My skin tingled as I shed my comforts and encountered experiences both thrilling and disquieting. I was curious to learn, but also anxious whenever I tried something new.

I remember venturing onto one food street, a potholed alleyway called Wujiang Lu packed with vendors grilling oysters, fish, tofu, and chicken wings, frying *sheng jian bao* (steamed then panfried soup dumplings), and serving slippery *suan la fen* (spicy and vinegary noodles made from sweet potato). As testament to the wave of progress in China,

The author marvels at the different mushroom varieties in Wuding, Yunnan.

Xinjiang kebabs from a bicycle-towed grill in Shanghai.

that potholed alleyway, once saturated with scents and drippings from night-market goodies, is today a cleaned-up walking street neatly lined with shops and kiosks. During its gritty days, my favorite spot for *sheng jian bao* was Xiao Yang Sheng Jian Bao, a crowded two-story joint with a long line streaming from its little doorway. You can now find the restaurant in a mall nearby, new and built to code. The lines are still long and the dumplings, thankfully, still divine.

Part of this change was spurred by the 2008 Beijing Olympics. The entire country was transforming. It was a very exciting time to be in China because the Olympics promised a new country, increasingly ready to face the world and anxious to share its history, culture, and business opportunities with the world. And the world was hungry to learn more about China and how to do business with its people. The Chinese were optimistic about the future, which hinted at the promise of a new prosperity and better quality of life. As an expat observer with friends in the hospitality, arts, and entertainment industries, I realized there wasn't a day that went by when someone wasn't creating, celebrating, or doing something inspiring. In fact, every person I met seemed to strike up interesting conversations that fueled creativity and drove curiosity.

The days that led up to the Beijing Olympics were never quiet. Everywhere I turned, the sounds and dust of construction filled the air, and there was always at least one crane in sight. The pace of construction was staggering. Buildings shot up like bamboo. The atmosphere was palpable with energy, and the celebrations were endless. I had the opportunity to eat at grand Chinese banquets and restaurants serving food that reflected the changing tastes of Beijing residents. But while my curiosity was piqued, I yearned to understand China at a deeper level, to see beyond restaurants and banquets popular among wealthier Chinese and foreigners—to experience real, off-the-beaten-path Chinese culture and food.

Specifically, I wanted to see Chinese family life, beyond Beijing and Shanghai. What did typical families eat? How did they live? My first visit to a family's home opened my eyes to a kitchen smaller than any I'd ever seen or used. The mother prepared five dishes, which we ate while seated on folding chairs in the living room. We reached for beer from the fridge located between the television and the front door. We finished with watermelon and grapes for dessert, then parted with a newfound hope for the future of humanity—a feeling I would experience over and over again after leaving different families' homes. I realized these simple experiences made me feel far more connected to people in China than I would ever feel traveling as a tourist.

Inspired to share my experiences with others, I created the blog *ShowShanti* to document the recipes and stories I collected from my time with families in both rural and urban parts of China. Looking back, I had little idea of the adventures that awaited, like unknowingly trying endangered black bear meat, or riding in fourth-class sleeper trains, faced with the gritty frankness of the human condition. Most memorably, I look back with fondness on the warm-hearted people who

shared their favorite foods in their homes and eateries, many of which no longer exist.

What makes the Chinese food experience so endearing? Well, if you've ever eaten with a Chinese family or in a Chinese restaurant, you've noticed that food isn't plated per person, but instead is presented on serving plates and shared by everyone. A meal is a communal affair, and everyone comes together with their chopsticks and bowl of rice to share the food. Family-style dining resonates throughout surrounding Asian countries, whose people have the same customary value of sharing food with others. It's how I eat everyday with my husband, Paul, and our son, Miles.

The communal meal isn't limited to families. I worked in a restaurant in Beijing, and when it was time for the staff to eat, the cooks prepared a couple of dishes and a pot of rice. Just before dinner service to customers began, the staff would eat together family style. I relished this opportunity to practice my Mandarin with the Chinese staff, and to learn more about everyone's backgrounds, culture, and daily lives.

In China, food brings people together. Certainly, family-style eating has an economical purpose, because sharing food within a group stretches limited resources for those on a lean budget, as many families have found throughout Chinese history. But there's so much more to it. Relationships cannot help but be fostered at a table where everyone shares the same food. Milestones are celebrated, honored guests are shown due respect, and although business isn't supposed to be discussed while eating, business deals are made after a business relationship has been nurtured at the table. For a brief and delicious moment, people forget their troubles, connecting and sharing through food.

Then there's the food itself. One rewarding characteristic of Chinese cooking is that after you prep—cut, chop, parboil, or mix—all that's left is to cook and serve. In this book, I'll share tips that I picked up for streamlining the prep work, and I'll present recipes that offer some of the basic flavors and ingredients that distinguish Chinese cuisine. You'll have fun trying the dishes and discovering your favorites.

Many families shared with me their own healthy habits, such as buying organic produce, never using monosodium glutamate (MSG), selecting locally sourced natural ingredients, and always cooking from scratch rather than buying processed foods. In my experience, Chinese families served loads of vegetables at every meal. And you'll find that this book doesn't have a dessert section, because after every meal, fresh fruit was normally served. Indeed, produce is pivotal in Chinese cooking—so have fun with it. Get to know your local farmers; visit farmers' markets, Asian groceries, and even the produce manager in your local supermarket. I love tossing seasonal produce into my wok after enhancing their flavors by using a combination of sauces (like my favorite, *dou ban jiang*—a spicy bean paste—with soy sauce).

Chinese cuisine is one of the richest in the world; I liken its complexity to French cooking. But don't let that discourage you—even I used to freeze up at the thought of cooking Chinese food. I'm not sure what courage potion I drank when I came up with the idea to travel through China and learn Chinese cooking armed only with my eyes, mouth, and broken Mandarin. I craved adventure, and yearned to explore the deeper culture and taste unusual and delicious foods. (Okay, I've stumbled upon some unsavory ones, too, some of which I will share.) Yes, the experience broke my fear of cooking Chinese food. But you don't need to travel the Far East to learn to cook that way. I'm bringing it to you.

Ready, set, *zuo fan* (start cooking)!

CHAPTER ONE

MY KITCHEN

When learning how to cook any new dish or cuisine, it helps to understand some basics. Here's one tip that helped me put my fears aside: Cooking Chinese home-style dishes is *simple* after all the preparation is done. Take this philosophy to heart, and you'll likely start cooking Chinese style out of convenience.

First, stock your kitchen with some basic sauces and spices (see page 18). Have dried mushrooms, scallions, ginger, and garlic handy. A fresh bell pepper, some celery and chiles, and a cut of pork or chicken are always good to have on hand. When it's time to cook, cut and prepare the ingredients as instructed and set them aside in prep bowls.

Chinese home cooking isn't fancy, and I love that about it. As I hovered over the shoulders of the home cooks who taught me their family recipes, they'd notice me converting their measures into teaspoons or tablespoons, and scrutinizing the amount of time for cooking. More than once I was told, "We Chinese do not cook with measurements. We cook with our hearts!" Once you become familiar with the proportions in these recipes, you, too, will start cooking with your heart.

CHINESE PANTRY STAPLES

When I lived in China, it wasn't hard to find most ingredients. If I needed something, I could simply bike to the closest neighborhood market to stalls selling specific ingredients. Noodles were always freshly made. I could tell the butcher the dish I was cooking, and he'd give me the cut of meat I would need. One of my favorite markets in Beijing was Sanyuanli. The diplomats' chefs shopped at this market for the freshest meats, seafood, and veggies before 10 a.m. I loved exploring that place! I'd find mushrooms from Yunnan, sand ginger from Guangdong, freshly pulled noodles and dumpling wrappers, live hairy crabs in season, and so much more. Since I couldn't drive in China, I only bought what I could carry on my bike. I can still remember the excitement of planning a dinner, then riding off to the market with my list.

In the United States, we don't always have the ready availability of the best Chinese ingredients. But the most important aspect to cooking a successful Chinese meal is freshness. This is especially important when you stock your pantry. You might find the Chinese ingredient you need in an Asian market like Ranch 99 (see Resources, page 174), but be sure to inspect the package carefully. Even in small shops in San Francisco's Chinatown I've found ingredients that were long expired. If your local store doesn't have an ingredient you need or if what they've got looks dodgy, try to buy it online. The staples listed here will help you cook the recipes in this book most authentically, and will also be useful for improvising when you want to cook seasonal vegetables with Chinese flavor. Don't be put off by the unfamiliar items: all ingredients used in these recipes can be bought either in a local Asian market or online. I promise you, stocking your pantry is the toughest part of cooking Chinese—once you've collected the ingredients, the rest is easy!

BLACK CARDAMOM Larger than green cardamom, this black aromatic pod (*cao guo*) about the size of a thumb is used for braising. In traditional Chinese culture, food is medicine. I learned how to make Braised Pork Ribs in Aromatic Sauce (page 111) in Sichuan, and the cook told me that black cardamom helps with digestion.

CASSIA BARK Also known as Chinese cinnamon, cassia bark is rougher and less red than cinnamon but the fragrance and flavor is similar. Be sure to buy the freshest you can, because stale cassia won't add life to a dish. If you can't find cassia bark, you can substitute cinnamon.

CHILI BEAN PASTE (*dou ban jiang*) This item is a must-have in your Chinese pantry. It is a rich, spicy, red chile paste blended with fermented broad beans. Just a tablespoon of the paste added to your stir-fry will elevate the dish. The best Chinese chili bean paste comes from Pi Xian in Sichuan province.

Top row, left to right: Black cardamom (cao guo); cassia bark; chili bean paste (dou ban jiang); chili oil. Bottom row, left to right: Chinese bacon (la rou); chinese cooking wine (liao jiu); cilantro.

CHILI OIL When made simply with red chile pepper flakes and hot oil, it is widely versatile for cooking or as a spicy condiment at the dining table. A more complex version of the oil can be made by adding ginger, garlic, whole chiles, and Sichuan peppercorns (see Scorched Chili Oil, page 37) or other aromatics that appeal to you.

CHINESE BACON The flavor of this cured meat depends on the region where it originates. I'll never forget the smoky flavor of the cold wind-dried pork belly often seen hanging from the balconies of homes in Sichuan, Yunnan, and Hunan. A few slices cut from this adds an irresistible umami to vegetable stir-fries and soups.

CHINESE COOKING WINE You'll see this ingredient again and again in the pages to come. Known as *liao jiu*, this rice wine comes in different grades, some that are used for drinking and some for cooking. A common type of Chinese cooking wine is called Shaoxing, named after a city in the Zhejiang province. If you can't find Shaoxing cooking wine, you can substitute a dry sherry. Cooking wine adds depth to the flavor of food and is especially useful in modifying the gaminess of meats like pork, chicken, and fish.

CHINKIANG VINEGAR This flavorful vinegar is easy to find online and at most Asian grocers. But in a pinch, you can substitute balsamic vinegar.

CILANTRO The Chinese name for this aromatic herb translates to "fragrant vegetable." In Western cooking, cilantro leaves are often the only part used for dishes. While helping to prep a meal in China, I was stopped just before discarding the stems, and was told that the fibrous stems possess even more flavor than their leafy offshoots.

COOKING OIL The recipes I learned in Sichuan and Inner Mongolia used rapeseed oil, which works well for cooking with high heat. But this oil isn't commonly available in the United States, and its health benefits are controversial. So I use peanut oil, avocado oil, or coconut oil to stir-fry over high heat.

CUMIN Originally from the Middle East, this spice used in Muslim ethnic cooking in the Xinjiang province has a distinctive, irresistible flavor. Walking through a night market in Kashgar, Chengdu, Xi'an, or Beijing, you might catch a whiff of lamb kebabs dusted with ground cumin, sesame seeds, red pepper flakes, and salt. There's something addictive about the way natural fats sizzle and mesh with the flavors of cumin and salt. And if you've never had the pleasure of having these kebabs in a Chinese night market, don't feel deprived—you can grill Xinjiang Lamb Kebabs at home (page 103).

DRIED RED CHILES Originally from Mexico, and Central and South America, chiles were introduced to China by Spanish and Portuguese traders. In Sichuan cuisine, red lantern chiles with a broad girth near the stem are used. More commonly found in mainland China and in the United States, are the longer, thinner red chiles.

DRIED SHIITAKE MUSHROOMS When you're making soup, fresh mushrooms lend a light flavor, while dried mushrooms impart a special taste attributed to their drying and decomposition. During a dinner at Yu's Family Kitchen in Chengdu, chef Yu Bo joined us after the meal and explained that he doesn't use monosodium glutamate (MSG) in his dishes because he is able to derive savory flavors from dried mushrooms, dried fish, and other dried ingredients. They are great to have on hand, and can be found at Asian grocery stores and many conventional supermarkets.

FERMENTED BEANS These pungent beans are soybeans or black beans that have been fermented without liquid. They impart a deep and earthy saltiness that complements other flavors in a dish. Asian delicacies like bitter melon are less bitter when stir-fried with fermented black beans. Fermented beans turn a simple bowl of steamed pork ribs into a lip-smacking delight. Before using them in a dish, soften the beans by soaking them in one of the liquids you'll be cooking with, whether it is water, broth, or something else. Add them to your dish early in the cooking process for a milder flavor with a light fragrance. For stronger flavor and fragrance, add them later. They can be bought at an Asian grocer or online.

FRESH CHILE PEPPERS In Sichuan and Hunan provinces, red and green chiles, long like ladies' fingers, are used regularly. The well-known dish Twice-Cooked Pork (page 113) uses a combination of sweet red chiles and spicy green chiles. Select fresh chile peppers that are in season at your local farmers' market, and experiment with their varied spiciness and sweetness. Seek out firm chiles, and store them in a paper bag in the refrigerator crisper.

Top row, left to right: Cumin, whole and ground; dried red chiles; dried shiitake mushrooms; fermented black beans.
Bottom row, left to right: Fresh chile peppers; ginger; pickled chiles; pickled dried mustard greens.

GARLIC Fresh garlic should be crisp and offer a pungent zing. Choose bulbs that are firm to the touch, and avoid those blackened from mold. Store in a dark, dry place. When preparing, you can easily peel a clove by smacking it with the flat side of your cleaver. Once smacked, the clove is also easy to slice or mince.

GINGER This medicinal rhizome is peppery, spicy, and fragrant. When a recipe calls for sliced or minced ginger, the thin brown skin should be removed with the edge of a spoon. When you're braising meat or making a soup, a knob of ginger can be smacked and the peel left on because it won't be eaten. Ginger is not only an essential flavor in many Chinese dishes, it is also used to dispel the gamey taste in raw meat. Select ginger that is firm and young because it has thinner, less

papery skin, and avoid any that shows mold or is shriveled.

PEANUT OIL Be sure to buy 100 percent peanut oil and not a blend. There is simply no substitute for the fragrance and flavor of pure peanut oil. The recipe for Sand Ginger Steamed Chicken (page 94) uses peanut oil. No other oil marries as well with sand ginger.

PICKLED CHILES Readily found packed in glass jars, this hot and salty condiment turns a simple steamed meat into an impressive dish. It also makes a great dipping sauce when mixed with soy sauce and vinegar.

PICKLED DRIED MUSTARD GREENS Don't be intimidated by the wilted, olive-green leaves, available in Asian markets and online. Across China, families have a string of salted mustard greens strewn outside their home, drying in the sun. Chop the greens and toss them into a stir-fry to bring out a bright flavor that opens the palate and appetite for more. You'll find this essential ingredient in Stir-Fried Pork with Pickled Mustard Greens (page 116).

POTATO STARCH This important ingredient serves two purposes in Chinese cooking. First, much like flour, it can serve as a sauce thickener. Second, in stir-fries it serves as a tenderizer for meat, poultry, or fish when added to marinades along with soy sauce, aromatics, and cooking wine. It helps to keep the meat moist while the protein absorbs the marinade. Potato starch can be found in most supermarkets.

RICE WINE VINEGAR Often used in Japanese cuisine, some Chinese families choose to use this type of vinegar in salads because it has a sweet flavor that eliminates the need to add sugar. It's particularly good with watermelon radish or daikon. This staple ingredient is easy to find at nearly any supermarket.

SAND GINGER Dried sand ginger can be found in Asian grocery stores. This is a relief, because I have looked for fresh sand ginger in supermarkets in the United States, without success. Even in Beijing, it was hard to find fresh sand ginger because it isn't typical in northern Chinese cuisines. Sand ginger is found mostly in Southeast Asian and Indian cuisines. I finally stumbled on the fresh version of this magical aromatic in Guangdong, in southern China.

SCALLIONS Whether you call it a scallion, spring onion, or green onion, you can use all parts of this onion to cook Chinese cuisine. The white part imparts the strong flavor and is generally used for cooking. The green part is most fragrant and often used to garnish a dish at the end of the cooking process.

SESAME OIL Sesame oil is made from toasted sesame seeds, and adds an alluring nutty fragrance in cold dishes and stir-fries. Sesame oil isn't meant to be cooked. Rather, it is drizzled sparingly on a dish just before serving. Like peanut oil, select a sesame oil that is pure (not a blend) for the best flavor. To ensure quality, store this oil (and all your oils) in a cool, dark location. Check for freshness and replace oils as needed.

What is Umami?

You'll see this word a lot in Chinese cooking. Umami is a fifth flavor after sweet, sour, bitter, and salty. Imagine salt with oomph—that's umami. You can find it by adding meat flavoring like chicken stock or by adding MSG. But it can also be added using dried mushrooms or fermented foods, because as food matures or decomposes like cheese, the flavors change to something that's often particularly enjoyable.

SICHUAN PEPPERCORNS Also known as "prickly ash," these berries are often mistaken for peppercorns, and their name doesn't help matters. Sichuan peppercorns are harvested in two different forms: red and green. The red peppercorns are the ones most commonly used in dishes and are known for their herbaceous, tingling, citrusy flavor. The green peppercorns are milder in flavor but produce a stronger fragrance. In the recipes in this book, use red Sichuan peppercorns unless the recipe states otherwise.

SOY SAUCE To explore Chinese cuisine, I encourage you to purchase both regular (light) and dark soy sauce, which have different uses. Regular soy sauce is saltier than dark soy sauce. Though dark soy sauce seems almost sinister in color, it is actually lighter in sodium but richer in flavor. Dark soy sauce also adds a deeper color to dishes. Tea Eggs (page 48) is one of several recipes that uses both light and dark soy sauce in their preparation.

STAR ANISE If you've had licorice, you know this flavor. Many Chinese braises, stews, and pickles wouldn't be what they are without this eight-pointed star spice. Much like cloves and cinnamon, this spice gives off a sweetly herbaceous and almost medicinal flavor. One star anise goes a long way, as is demonstrated in a pot of Braised Pork Ribs in Aromatic Sauce (page 111).

Top row, left to right: Soy sauce; star anise; sweet noodle sauce; wood ear mushrooms.
Bottom row, left to right: Potato starch; sand ginger; scallion; Sichuan peppercorn.

SUGAR Despite its less-than-healthy reputation, it's important to not banish this staple from the kitchen and to simply use it wisely. Food must have a balance of flavors and sweet is an important part of that mix. A teaspoon of sugar in a stir-fry serving four is not excessive, and it will add good flavor.

SWEET NOODLE SAUCE This sweet and savory sauce is made from fermented flour, salt, and water. Also called *tian mian jiang*, it is best known for its use in traditional Chinese mixed-sauce noodles. It's widely available at Asian grocers and online (see Resources, page 174).

WOOD EAR MUSHROOMS These mushrooms are also known as black fungus or cloud ear fungus. They are available fresh at Asian grocers; otherwise they are sold dried in stores or online. Dried wood ear mushrooms should be soaked in warm water for 20 minutes, then rinsed and trimmed of any hard bits like the stem. They can be sliced or torn into pieces, depending on the recipe. If not available, you can use shiitakes or simply leave them out. But I do like them for their crunchy texture.

Core Flavors

Chinese cooking often refers to the "core flavors" or "five flavors." The five core flavors in traditional Chinese dishes are spicy, salty, sweet, sour, and bitter. When you dine with Chinese friends, you may notice that unlike Western meals, the sweet dish doesn't necessarily come at the end. Instead, the entire meal is a journey of flavors and textures. This journey may open up with a cold and sour dish, tantalize with a spicy stir-fry, warm with bitter melon in black bean sauce, sweeten with fresh fruits, and then close with a savory fish steamed with soy sauce. There isn't any specific order; the journey changes every time.

You can achieve the Chinese-style core flavors at home. Just keep your pantry stocked with soy sauce, fermented soybeans, chili bean paste, sweet noodle sauce, sugar, black vinegar, and Shaoxing cooking wine (or dry sherry) for depth of flavor. To supply the bitter note, you can fix a dish of bitters using radish, kale, cabbage, bitter melon (Asian grocers carry this), and other vegetables. Complement the bitter veggies with the savory sauces in your pantry.

ESSENTIAL EQUIPMENT

Many kitchens in China are so small, at first I wondered how anyone could cook in them. The kitchens of my rental apartments in China were the size of a small bathroom. Most stoves had only two burners and rarely an oven. If anyone had an oven, it was a countertop convection oven, and the owner had a passion for baking Western desserts. But I quickly learned that cooking home-style Chinese dishes requires few utensils. You, too, will soon understand how most Chinese kitchens get away with being spartan.

CLEAVER You can do all your prep with just one cleaver. There are heavy cleavers for breaking through rib bones, but a common, lighter cleaver, the *cai dao* (literally meaning vegetable knife), can finely slice scallion slivers and break down a chicken equally well. A few households I visited had two cleavers—one for cutting meat and another just for vegetables. Your common cleaver shouldn't weigh a ton, as you'll need the lightness for cutting vegetables quickly and with ease.

CUTTING BOARD Choose a wooden board that's heavy enough not to slide around. I like to place a damp tea towel under my cutting board for extra stability. Nothing fancy required—some homes I visited had a six-inch slice of tree trunk for a chopping block!

GLAZED CLAY POT These pots are used for braising and stewing. It is important to warm this pot slowly using a low heat setting at first, then gradually increase to medium heat. Sudden or high heat will crack the pot. I broke many clay pots before understanding this rule. If you don't have a glazed clay pot, invest in a Dutch oven.

LADLE A ladle is especially useful for removing excess liquid from a stir-fry or scooping stock or water from a pot into the wok. It's also handy for serving soup into small bowls.

MANDOLINE This slicer is optional and not necessarily a Chinese tool, but many households I visited in China used them, and I became a convert. When you've got a party of eight for dinner and eight dishes to prep for, the mandoline will make quick work of your labor.

PREP BOWLS There's a lot of cutting in Chinese cooking. I like to have at least eight metal bowls for keeping cut-and-measured ingredients in. When it's time to stir-fry, having all the ingredients ready to toss in as if you're a cooking show host is very convenient.

RICE COOKER Rice cookers are handy because after the rice is measured, washed, and soaked, you can just turn on the cooker and wait for it to turn off automatically once it's done. You don't have to watch the pot the

way you have to watch a pot of rice cooking on the stove top. Rice cookers come in various sizes and can also cook other dishes, like my favorite Sand Ginger Steamed Chicken (page 94), which calls for a large rice cooker big enough to cook a five-pound chicken! Just like when cooking rice, the cooker automatically turns off when the food is done.

SPIDER If you've ever tried to fish for spaghetti in a pot of boiling water, you'll understand why this tool is so useful. Whether it's parboiling vegetables, boiling noodles, skimming scum from the surface of boiling meat, or deep-frying, this wire mesh ladle will capture elusive food with ease.

STEAMER You may have seen small bamboo steamers stacked on carts in a dim sum restaurant—they look like hat boxes. This cooking vessel steams food, retaining nutrients and eliminating the need for cooking oils. I prefer steamers made from bamboo because the wood imparts a lovely fragrance. For a 14-inch wok, fit a 12-inch steamer within it, and layer on one to two baskets when steaming; any more and the top basket might not receive enough steam. You can also use a wire steamer rack that fits in the wok.

TONGS Many Chinese families use giant chopsticks for serving, but I prefer the stability of silicone-tipped tongs, which are great for grasping long vegetables or large chunks of meat when parboiling. Sometimes it's hard to stir-fry a mound of cut kale or long green beans, and tongs help with turning the ingredients evenly and quickly. When steaming small bowls in the steamer, I find the silicone tips have a more secure grip for lifting them out.

WOK Traditional Chinese kitchens have stove tops with a hole that accommodates a curved-bottom wok. Below the hole, the flame—wood fire or gas—heats the wok. But you don't need this. I recommend what I was taught: Use a cast iron (or carbon steel) wok or skillet, because it conducts

heat most evenly, and with time and care, a well-seasoned wok forms a patina of oil that prevents ingredients from sticking. If you have a gas stove top with grates, you may be able to set your curve-bottomed wok easily upon it. But if not, you can find a wok ring to place atop your gas-burning stove top to keep your wok stable. If you don't have a gas flame to cook on, you can buy a portable burner to set on your countertop. If you have a glass stove top, an electric burner, or a mild burning flame at high, a portable burner is a great option, because stir-frying is best over the high heat it can provide.

WOK SPATULA Look for a wok spatula with a curved edge that matches the curve of the wok's bottom. With the flick of a wrist or a good scooping gesture, you'll have better control of your stir-fry than you would with any other tool. In China, the wok spatula was often used to quickly "measure" oil or sauces before adding them to the wok.

At the Chinese Table

In Chinese culture, there are many rules to remember, depending on the situation. My mother always told me, when you're unsure about what to do at a table, observe others. And as with any culture, you can't go wrong by simply being courteous, serving those to the left and right of you, respecting your elders, and eating at a respectable pace.

Wait to be seated. When you eat at a Chinese home or at a Chinese banquet, do not sit until you've been assigned. Typically, the guest of honor will sit directly across the table from the entrance, and the host will sit closest to the door.

Serve others first. Food is served family style. Try to serve those to your left and right before helping yourself. There may be a bowl of rice on a plate accompanied by chopsticks. In a familiar setting, everyone will use their personal pair of chopsticks to help each other and themselves from the plates of food. But in a more formal setting, there may be communal chopsticks and spoons used for serving.

Spoon, chopstick, or neither? When the soup arrives, it will be served into small bowls. Soup spoons are typically used when eating soup noodles served in larger bowls. Chopsticks are most easily used with the dominant hand, and the other hand can use a spoon to sip soup or steady a dumpling. However, when you simply have broth in a small bowl, you can bring the bowl up to your lips, with elbows down (not at your ears), and sip softly, allowing air to pass with the soup between your lips to cool it while drinking.

Trust your host's rations. You needn't worry about a shortage of food, because your host will have artfully ordered or provided the right dishes and amount. A home cook strives to honor a guest with more food than can actually be eaten. A rule of thumb for the host is to serve one dish for every guest at the table. A Chinese banquet will serve nine dishes—the number nine symbolizes eternity and completeness.

Don't fix perfection. If you've ever seen the film *The Joy Luck Club*, you might remember the faux pas made by the Westerner as he doused a homemade dish made by the host with soy sauce. No matter how much you love a condiment, I advise refraining so you don't insult your host.

In family-style meals, a Chinese home cook aims to offer more food than will likely be eaten.

Pour or tap. Whoever sits closest to the tea or other beverages customarily serves others and is expected to observe their cups and keep them filled. If someone pours for you, you can say thank you, but if you're mid-conversation, you can tap your index finger and middle finger together against the table. This quick and casual gesture actually alludes to a story about Emperor Qian Long, who disguised himself as a commoner and went outside the palace walls with his servant. After he poured his servant a drink, the servant wanted to show respect without kowtowing, so he used his two knuckles to tap the table as if kneeling in gratitude. You may use your knuckles as the servant did, or simply tap the tips of your fingers.

Cheers with respect. There will likely be toasting. Whether you drink alcohol or not is up to you. Women are typically served less alcohol and not expected to drink as much as the men. Everyone will cheer "*Gan bei!*" which literally translates to "dry cup." Upon toasting, you may be expected to empty your glass, but if you fear getting sick or losing your sobriety, it's okay to just sip with each toast instead. A unique but important rule when you toast your glass against another: Do your best to position your glass to clink at the lower half of the other person's glass. This is a sign of respect, especially with elders and dignitaries. And at more formal dinners, be sure to hold your glass with two hands.

Top to bottom: Sichuan crayfish restaurateur Jiang Yi shows the author how to eat a whole eel. Author toasts Han Ayi with Yanjing beer; her glass tipped to clink lower than her host's glass.

BASIC COOKING TECHNIQUES

As you read through the following cooking techniques, you may feel relieved by how simple it sounds. And it is! As mentioned earlier, the most challenging aspect of Chinese home-style cooking is sourcing the ingredients. Once you've got the goods and they're prepped, the cooking is surprisingly easy and quick.

Cutting

Preparing the ingredients for your dishes will involve a lot of cutting. The shape matters, since it affects not only the aesthetic presentation but also how evenly your food will cook with the other ingredients. Here are some basic cuts used in this book:

1. JULIENNE Slice into thin strips, from matchstick size (slivers) to fajita-strip size.

2. MINCE Finely chop by first slicing, then slivering, and finally cross-cutting the slivers into tiny bits.

3. SLICE Thinly cut vegetables or meat with a cleaver into pieces ⅛ to ¼ inch thick, depending on the ingredient. With vegetables, the mandoline comes in handy for efficiency and size consistency.

4. HORSE EARS Slice long ingredients like celery or scallions at a sharp angle, into thin slices that resemble the ears of a horse.

5. SLIVERS Thinly slice a vegetable, then slice each piece again into thin pieces the size of matchsticks, creating a thin julienne.

6. SMACK Take the flat side of your cleaver, hold it against the ginger root, cucumber, or garlic clove, and firmly whack the cleaver with the heel of your hand. If you smack too hard, however, you may find pieces flying.

7. STRIPS Achieved by slicing the ingredient (like tofu) thickly, then cutting each slice once again to create thinner strips.

8. CUBES Taking the strips one step further, this involves cutting a strip of meat or tofu across into small cubes.

Tenderizing Meat

When stir-frying chicken, beef, or pork, potato starch helps tenderize the meat. Slice or julienne the meat, then toss it with a marinade that includes a teaspoonful of potato starch. The protein will absorb the flavors while the starch locks in the moisture. Corn starch or tapioca starch can also be used if potato starch isn't available. But when using starch as a tenderizer, limit marinating time of the meat to less than 20 minutes or it may get too dry.

Stir-Frying

This method uses a small amount of oil to cook small cuts of food over medium heat until the liquid has mostly evaporated and the food has become fragrantly toasted. Sauces and aromatic veggies are added near the end so their flavor remains robust.

You may have heard that stir-frying is healthy. This is true, but there are a few guidelines. Make sure the heat is at its highest. A round-bottomed cast iron or carbon-steel wok conducts heat well and evenly. The rounded bottom will allow you to quickly toss the meat and vegetables with a round-edged spatula. As long as your wok is well-seasoned, a little cooking oil will suffice, and food won't stick. And, if you cut the vegetables and meat the same size and stir-fry in separate phases (vegetables first, then meat, then return the veggies to the stir-fry), you'll reduce the cooking time and ensure that the food retains most of its nutrients.

Cutting all ingredients to size and parboiling when necessary can make prep time considerable, but once all items are ready, the stir-fry part of the process is quick. For this reason, I like to prep everything before guests arrive to a dinner party. Once every guest has arrived, I quickly stir-fry all the dishes and serve them hot.

Julia Child liked to say, "Don't crowd the mushrooms!" This rule also applies to anything in a stir-fry. If there's too much food in the wok, it will wilt and lack crispness, and the meat won't have enough heat to brown. Stir-frying food in phases helps to cook

Seasoning Your Wok

Before you use a new carbon-steel or cast-iron wok, take the time to season it. For a brand-new wok, first wash it with dish soap to remove substances from manufacturing. Dry the wok with a paper towel, and heat it on the stove top over medium heat for five minutes. Add a few tablespoons of cooking oil to the wok and swirl it around to coat the surface. Slice a knob of ginger and stir-fry the pieces for several minutes. Discard the oil and ginger, then wipe the surface of all excess oil. Add oil to a paper towel and wipe the surface of the wok again. In the future, after cooking with the wok, wash with water only, and use plain steel wool (plain, not Brillo or SOS) for any stubborn bits of food.

Other important tips:

- After the first wash of a new wok, never use soap on the wok again.

- Never stick your wok in the dishwasher, since the high heat and soap will dry out the iron, cause rust, and require a re-seasoning.

- After a boil or stew, the surface will need to be re-seasoned.

- To re-season a wok, apply oil to a paper towel and rub the inside surface of the dry wok. Heat the wok on the stove top until the oil begins to smoke. Cool, then wipe with a clean paper towel.

- Store the wok so that dust doesn't stick to the seasoned surface. I store my wok inside my oven or upside down on top of my stove. Upside down in a cabinet works too.

- An electric wok works as an alternative. In fact, a family I visited in Shandong used one.

- A cast iron skillet is a good wok substitute. It heats well and evenly and can be used on any cooking surface.

everything for the right amount of time. At the end, return each ingredient to the wok for a warming toss together without overcooking.

Steaming

Another healthy method for cooking food is steaming. This option doesn't require oil, except perhaps a drizzle of sesame oil just for flavor. When you steam food in a bamboo steamer or wok, be sure to steam the food in a heatproof dish that will fit inside once the lid goes on.

Parboiling or Blanching

Some ingredients benefit from being cooked a little before being added to a stir-fry. Parboiling helps to soften denser meats and vegetables. Blanching is parboiling followed by a dunk in ice water to stop cooking. Watch vegetables carefully while parboiling, because they can easily overcook. This process is also useful for removing impurities from meats before adding them to a soup or braise.

Braising

Braising involves a quick, light fry in a little bit of oil, then stewing slowly in a closed container. There are many ways to braise in Chinese cookery, but the braising recipes in this book do best in a covered clay pot or Dutch oven over very low heat. Some popular braising methods include:

DRY-BRAISING This method is used mostly for fish and seafood. The protein is simmered in the sauce of choice over medium heat in a clay pot or Dutch oven until the liquid reduces to a thicker sauce. Some water may be added in order to prevent scorching.

RED-COOKING (ALSO CALLED RED-BRAISING) Here, the protein is parboiled, then slow-cooked in a soy sauce base liquid with additional flavorings of aromatic spices and stocks. Meat such as pork can be slow-cooked for 1 to 2 hours; fish should be cooked no more than 20 minutes using this method to prevent overcooking.

Family-Style Servings

You'll notice that some of my recipes offer yields or serving sizes and some do not. As the dishes are intended to be served family style, it's hard to predict how many guests one fish or a vegetable stir-fry will serve. When serving a Chinese meal, it is important to have more than enough food for your guests. A good rule of thumb is to have at least one dish per guest.

For a party of four, I open with a cold dish like Fern Root Noodle Salad (page 77), then a couple of meat entrées like Crispy Chicken and Red Chiles (page 86) and Old Wife Ma Po's Tofu (page 110), two vegetable stir-fries, and steamed rice. For a party of six, I may add an appetizer and finish with a soup. And as they do China, I serve seasonal fruit at the very end.

THE BASICS

Scorched Chile Oil (page 37)

STEAMED RICE

Zhēng Mǐ Fàn 蒸米饭

Rice. We like eating it, but cooking it is another story. It's overcooked, it's under-cooked, it sticks to the pan. No more! My advice for cooking perfectly steamed rice: buy a rice cooker. A simple one isn't expensive, and it will save you the drudgery of watching the rice while you could be focused on creating the other exciting dishes in a meal. YIELD: SERVES 2 TO 3

For two people, add 1 cup uncooked rice to the pot. Wash the rice under cold water, drain, and rinse a couple of times or until the water is nearly clear. Level the rice in the pot with your fingers, and add enough water to meet the first joint line of your index finger. (If you are cooking brown rice, use your middle finger.) Let the rice soak for at least 1 hour. If possible, let the rice soak covered in the refrigerator for 6 hours or even over-night (see Cooking Tip).

When you're ready to cook, place the pre-soaked rice into the cooker, cover, and press "Start." When the rice is done, the cooker will shut off automatically.

If using the stove top, bring the rice to a boil, then reduce the heat to low and cover. If you have soaked it, it should only need to simmer for 10 to 15 minutes. The steam will cause little pockets to form on the surface once the rice is ready. Remove the rice from the heat and fluff with a fork. Keep covered until ready to serve.

COOKING TIP: Taking the time to soak the rice helps soften it and reduce cooking time. After you've washed and soaked the rice, don't drain the water; rather, use that same water for cooking. Also, neglect the rice. Yes, really! Leave the rice undisturbed while it is cooking. Too much handling or stirring can result in soggy or broken rice.

SCORCHED CHILI OIL

Hóng Yóu 红油

FAMILY: HAN XIANMING 韩先明 | TONGZHOU, BEIJING

As you begin cooking Chinese, I encourage you to start off with this recipe. Scorched Chili Oil is a staple used in many of the recipes in this book and is specified to be served with or without sediment. The sediment means the ground red pepper flakes in the oil. This versatile oil is good sprinkled over eggs, tossed into fried rice, drizzled on grilled meats, or added to a stir-fry. Because this gorgeous, fiery oil has a nutty flavor you just can't get in store-bought chili oils, it's best to make your own oil fresh. Keep it on hand to cook with and offer it as a condiment for meals. It also makes a lovely gift for friends who are into spices. **YIELD: MAKES 1 CUP**

½ cup ground red pepper flakes

8 to 10 whole dried red chiles

1 (1-inch) piece fresh ginger, sliced

1 teaspoon Sichuan peppercorns

2 to 3 cloves garlic, sliced (optional)

¾ cup peanut oil

In a heat-proof bowl, add the red pepper flakes, whole red chiles, ginger, peppercorns, and garlic (if using).

Heat the peanut oil in a medium saucepan until it reaches 250°F. (To test temperature if you don't have a deep-fry thermometer, when the oil starts to shimmer, drop a Sichuan peppercorn, chile pepper, or sliver of garlic into the oil to see if bubbles appear.)

Remove the saucepan from the heat. Pour the oil into the bowl with the chili mixture to scorch the chiles. The mixture will sizzle and fill the air with a spicy, nutty fragrance.

Let the chili oil cool. Remove the ginger and garlic pieces and discard. Store the chili oil in an airtight jar in a cool place or in the refrigerator.

VARIATION TIP: Give the chili oil your own signature style by adding star anise, cassia bark, bay leaves, cloves, or other types of dried chiles.

REAL CHINA—MY FIRST VISIT TO A CHINESE HOME

In China, *ayi* (meaning "auntie") is a term of endearment and respect for a woman. It is common for someone who manages the cooking, children, and household to be referred to as Ayi. Han Ayi used to come to my home from Monday to Friday to clean, sometimes cook, and chat with me. When I was sick, she cared for me. She was essentially my mom away from home. One of the things that drew me to her was her cooking. When my ayi cooked something tasty for me, she told me she'd show me how to make it. It was fitting that my journey to the kitchens of Chinese families began at Han Ayi's apartment in the suburb of Tongzhou, just outside of Beijing.

It was a Saturday morning. Ayi's husband picked Peikwen and me up at my apartment in Beijing. Forty-five minutes later, we arrived in a neighborhood of six-story buildings with no elevators. After climbing four flights of stairs, we were greeted by Ayi's son, Gao Jia, who opened the door to their sunlit home. Two steps from the threshold a rabbit called Dandan—dan meaning "egg"—sat in a cage. Piles of stuffed animals lined the floor from the living room to the bedroom, and pet turtles and fish purchased in twos filled the home with the playful charm I could detect in my ayi's daily chatter.

In the four-by-six-foot kitchen, I watched in awe as Ayi tossed vegetables and meats into a hissing wok. Spices and sauces crackled as they joined each stir-fry. While I had only asked to learn two or three recipes, she pivoted about the floor whipping up six dishes on the two-burner stove typical of most mainland Chinese homes.

Ayi showed me how to cook each dish with the pride of a parent imparting a valuable gift or lesson to their child. Ayi was cooking a lamb dish with scallions—one of Gao Jia's favorites. In fact, he refused to order this dish in restaurants, feeling any other version paled in comparison to his mother's. Another dish, one that I had never encountered in American Chinese restaurants, was Fern Root Noodle Salad (page 77)—a fresh salad confettied with carrots, blanched red cabbage, cilantro, garlic, and cucumber. As each dish was brought out of the kitchen and scooped

This page: Han Ayi, Gao Shushu, Gao Jia, and the author at her first family visit to learn Chinese cooking.

Opposite, clockwise: Han Ayi, the author's first teacher in Chinese cooking. The fresh ingredients for Han Ayi's Fern Root Noodle Salad. Tossing the salad in its sesame dressing. Gao Shushu pours a stiff celebratory glass of baijiu, a medicinal-flavored rice wine.

carefully into serving plates, Ayi made sure I tasted each one while it was hot and at its best.

We set up the folding card table and stools between the front door and the television. Then we set out plastic cups, a couple room-temperature bottles of Yanjing beer, and a meal so copious it barely fit on the table.

Halfway through our meal, Ayi's husband, Gao Shushu, who was also full of smiles and as welcoming a host as his wife, reached for a bottle of hard stuff. What better way to christen my first family visit than with *baijiu*? This stiff Chinese rice wine has medicinal fumes that linger from the palate to the gut. As is common for most Chinese meals, our lunch concluded with a much-welcomed plate of watermelon slices. The fruit soothed the burn from the *baijiu*, cooled the spices, and seemingly washed away the oils.

As I did my best to observe, learn, and document, I found myself brimming with certainty that I had finally found my dream project. In fact, I felt like I was dreaming, but luckily I have photos to prove it really happened. This was the China I had traveled across the ocean to find. A little more modern than the China of author Pearl S. Buck, but as down to earth as I'd hoped. This was one of many experiences my fiancé and I had hoped to encounter—a simple family meal shared with a local family. And this one was special, because it was with our surrogate family. Ayi took great care of us until she retired in her late 50s. Her son Gao Jia assisted me in the first months of my project. And just like the gifts that parents give us, we moved away but still keep some useful and hopefully delicious tools for survival.

CHICKEN STOCK

Jī Tāng 鸡汤

We're learning that the less processed food is, the better it is for our health. Nearly every family I met in China used powdered chicken bouillon and/or MSG for extra umami. Some families didn't usually use MSG, but would add it to dishes when cooking for guests. You may look at a jar of chicken bouillon and not see MSG as an ingredient, but instead see "natural flavors" or "natural flavoring," which is vague. The best way to ensure the integrity of your food and health is to make it yourself. Chicken stock is one of those ingredients that can be made easily from scratch, you control the ingredients, and you can make it in batches to always have on hand.

YIELD: 4 QUARTS (16 CUPS)

1 whole chicken (organic, if possible), cut into pieces or left whole if small

8 scallions, cut into 2-inch pieces

1 (1-inch) piece peeled fresh ginger, smacked with the side of a cleaver blade

6 whole garlic cloves

½ cup Shaoxing cooking wine or dry sherry

Place the chicken into a stockpot, and add enough water to cover. Bring the water to a boil over high heat and cook for 5 minutes. Drain and discard the liquid. Rinse the chicken parts of any residue.

Return the chicken to the stockpot and add the scallions, ginger, garlic, wine, and 4 quarts of water. Bring the stock to a simmer. Without stirring the stock, skim off the residue that surfaces with a slotted spoon until the stock looks clear. Reduce the heat to low and simmer for 2 to 4 hours.

Remove the chicken and other solids and discard. Strain the liquid through a fine-mesh strainer. Line the strainer with a paper towel or a thin cloth for even finer straining. Let the stock cool, then store in the refrigerator in an airtight container for up to 5 days. Alternatively, freeze stock in an ice cube tray and add a cube to your dishes as needed instead of bouillon.

VARIATION TIP: Add a handful of dried shiitake or vegetable scraps from previous meals. Scraps can be sealed in a plastic bag and stored in the freezer until it's time to make a batch of stock.

COOKING TIP: Keep the stock at a simmer, not a boil, or the fats will disperse in the liquid and make a cloudy, less healthy stock.

MUNG BEAN NOODLES

Liángfěn 凉粉

When I think of foods that were easy to find in China but are nowhere to be found in the United States, my heart aches a little with nostalgia. One of those foods is the cool, slippery-smooth yet firm mung bean jelly cut into strips and served as a cold-noodle appetizer. Mung beans are small green legumes, and in China mung bean jelly is sold in boxes much like tofu. You can slice this tasty, fiber-rich product, cut it into strips, or cube it, then toss it with a savory chili bean sauce. Luckily, the ingredients can be purchased online or in an Asian grocery, so you can give it a try. **YIELD: 6 SERVINGS**

½ cup mung bean starch

¼ teaspoon sea salt

In a medium pot, combine the mung bean starch, 3½ cups of water, and salt, and mix well with a wooden spoon. Bring the mixture to a gentle boil over medium heat, and cook for 10 minutes, stirring occasionally to prevent sticking. Lower the heat to low and simmer for 3 minutes. The consistency should be thick and translucent like a liquid paste. Remove from the heat.

Pour the mixture into one (13-by-9-inch) or two (8-by-8-inch) glass baking dishes and cool. Seal with plastic wrap, and chill in the refrigerator for 3 to 4 hours. The mixture will gel.

When ready to slice, use a spatula to loosen the jelly from the sides of the dish. Flip the dish upside down, letting the jelly fall onto the cutting board. Cut the jelly into strips.

To serve, dress with your desired sauce.

COOKING TIP: The square or rectangular glass baking dishes are recommended for ease of cutting noodles into straight lines, which is hard to do with a round or oval container.

DUMPLING WRAPPERS

Jiǎo Zi Pí 饺子皮

Dumpling wrappers might be available in your local supermarket, but just in case you can't find them, it's good to know that you can easily make them yourself. You'll just need a little elbow grease, patience, and maybe a helper. YIELD: MAKES 35 TO 40 WRAPPERS

4 cups all-purpose flour, plus more for dusting

½ teaspoon sea salt

On a large, smooth work surface, put the flour in a mound with the salt, then make a well in the center. With one hand, slowly pour 1⅓ cups of cold water into the well while mixing the flour into the water with the other hand. Aim for a dough that is slightly firmer than pizza dough but moister than pie dough. Knead for about 10 minutes, until smooth. Cover the dough with a damp towel and let it rest for 30 minutes.

Roll the dough out into long sausage shapes about 2 inches thick. Pull off pieces of dough slightly smaller than a Ping-Pong ball, and roll them on the counter to make a ball. Flatten them with your palm.

Using a flour-dusted rolling pin or bottle, press each disk into 3-inch pancakes. Stack them as you make them, dusting with flour to prevent sticking.

COOKING TIP: Store the wrappers in a sealed container and keep in the refrigerator for 3 or 4 days. Allow the dough to come to room temperature before using.

HANDMADE NOODLES

Shǒu Gǎn Miàn 手擀面

Whenever I think of noodles—beyond their satisfying chewiness and the joy of watching my son chew and feed strands into his mouth simultaneously—I think of their symbolic meaning of long life, and their special place on Chinese birthday menus. Because noodles represent longevity, Chinese tradition says you never want to cut them. Fresh handmade noodles are easy to make and a treat to eat. Top them with the Shanghai specialty Eight-Treasure Spicy Sauce (page 64), or use them to make an umami-loaded bowl of Beijing-Style Noodles (page 168). YIELD: SERVES 8

5 cups all-purpose flour, plus more for dusting

1 egg, beaten

½ teaspoon sea salt

Sesame oil

STORAGE TIP: Keep unused noodles in an airtight container in the refrigerator for up to 3 days.

VARIATION TIP: If you want the noodles to be a little more chewy, add an additional beaten egg. For softer noodles, add an additional ¼ cup of water.

In a large bowl, mix together the flour, 2 cups of water, egg, and salt. Knead the mixture into a dough.

Transfer the dough to a work surface, and continue kneading until very smooth with no visible air pockets or bubbles. Cover the dough with a damp towel and let rest for about 30 minutes.

Knead the dough thoroughly again, then shape it into a ball. Dust a cutting board or smooth work surface with flour. Using a rolling pin, roll out the dough as thinly as possible. This is most easily done by rolling out the dough in sections and folding the section on itself, until all the dough is rolled out to about ⅛ inch thickness.

Using a sharp knife, cut the folded dough into thin strips. If you like wider noodles, cut them to the width of your preference. Dust the strips with flour and loosen them from the work surface. When ready to use, bring a pot of water to a boil over high heat, add the noodles, reduce the heat to medium-low, and simmer for 3 to 4 minutes. Drain in a colander, and rinse with cold water.

In a large bowl, toss the noodles with 1 teaspoon sesame oil, or more if desired, to help keep the noodles separated and to add lovely flavor to them.

SICHUAN CHILI BEAN STIR-FRY SAUCE

Dòu Bàn Jiàng 豆瓣酱

Try this sauce with okra, Chinese eggplant, cauliflower, green beans, or mustard greens. Known in Mandarin as *dou ban jiang*, chili bean sauce is a fermented blend of broad beans and chiles. This savory, spicy sauce from Sichuan can be found in most Asian grocers and in some conventional supermarkets in the Asian food aisle. Look for the Lee Kum Kee brand.

1 tablespoon peanut oil

1 (1-inch) piece peeled fresh ginger, sliced

1 to 2 cloves garlic, smacked and sliced

1 teaspoon Sichuan peppercorns

1 tablespoon chili bean paste

1 tablespoon soy sauce

Sea salt

1 teaspoon sesame oil, for serving

Heat the oil in a wok over high heat. Add the ginger, garlic, and Sichuan peppercorns, and stir-fry until fragrant, about 10 seconds.

Add the vegetables. Stir-fry for 1 to 2 minutes. Add the chili bean paste and soy sauce. Season with salt. Stir-fry until the greens are just tender.

Drizzle with sesame oil and serve.

Quick Stir-Fry Sauces

Keeping some basic ingredients (page 18) in your pantry will ensure that you're ready to make authentic Chinese food at a moment's notice. The sauces on pages 44 and 45 can be added to a meat, fish, or vegetable/tofu stir-fry. These recipes make the right amount for 1 bunch of your favorite leafy greens like kale or Swiss chard or 1 pound baby spinach. When you wash leafy greens, particularly the ones with woody stems like kale and chard, don't dry the water off. The drops of water help to soften them. See what is seasonal at your local farmers' market, and try these sauces on fresh produce.

GARLIC AND CHILI OIL

Suàn Róng Là Jiāo Yóu 蒜蓉辣椒油

Try this sauce in a stir-fry containing napa cabbage, sliced zucchini, sliced portabello mushrooms, oyster mushrooms, or even slivered potatoes.

1 tablespoon peanut oil

2 to 3 cloves garlic, smacked and sliced

2 to 3 dried red chiles, broken in two

1 teaspoon Sichuan peppercorns (optional)

1 tablespoon Scorched Chili Oil with sediment (page 37)

Sea salt

Heat the oil in a wok over high heat. Add the garlic, dried chiles, and Sichuan peppercorns (if using), and stir-fry until fragrant, about 10 seconds.

Add the vegetables. Stir-fry for 1 to 2 minutes. Add the scorched chili oil. Season with salt. Stir-fry until the greens are just tender.

Drizzle with sesame oil, and serve.

BLACK BEAN STIR-FRY SAUCE

Bào Chǎo Dòu Chǐ 爆炒豆豉

Try this sauce with Chinese eggplant, broccoli, bitter melon, Brussels sprouts, asparagus, broccoli rabe, or green beans.

1 tablespoon peanut oil

1 to 2 cloves garlic, smacked and sliced

1 teaspoon fermented black beans (page 20)

1 teaspoon sesame oil, for serving

Heat the oil in a wok over high heat. Add the garlic and stir-fry until fragrant, about 10 seconds.

Before stir-frying, soften the black beans in warm water for 5 minutes, then drain and chop.

Add the vegetables. Stir-fry for 1 to 2 minutes. Add the black beans. Season with salt. Stir-fry until the greens are just tender.

Drizzle with sesame oil and serve.

APPETIZERS
& SIDE DISHES

Tea Eggs (page 48)

TEA EGGS

Chá Yè Dàn 茶叶蛋

In China, the ever-present tea eggs can be found in snack stalls, steeping away in a pot at the morning *jian bing* (egg crêpe) cart. Walk into any 7-Eleven (yes, China has them too!) and there they sit in lidded electric pots competing with the other salty snacks. The trifecta of hard-boiled egg, soy sauce, and the broth's aromatic spices makes them an irresistible make-at-home snack.

¼ cup Shaoxing cooking wine or dry sherry

2 tablespoons soy sauce

2 tablespoons dark soy sauce

3 tablespoons loose black tea leaves

1 whole star anise

1 (2-inch) piece cassia bark or cinnamon bark

1 teaspoon sugar

8 large eggs

To make tea broth, in a medium pot over medium-high heat, combine the wine, soy sauce, dark soy sauce, tea leaves, star anise, cassia bark, sugar, and 3 of cups water. Bring just to a simmer, stirring frequently. Reduce the heat to low and simmer for 30 minutes. Strain the broth through a fine-mesh sieve into another medium pot, discard the solids, and return the broth to the medium pot.

Put the eggs in a large saucepan over medium-high heat, and cover with water by 1 inch. Bring to a boil. Reduce the heat to low and simmer for 8 minutes. Drain and discard the water.

Using the back of a spoon, gently tap the shells of the eggs so they are cracked all over. Do not peel the eggs; they should look like they are webbed with cracks.

Put the cracked eggs in the pot of tea broth over medium-high heat, and bring just to a boil. Reduce the heat to low, and simmer for 30 to 40 minutes. Remove from the heat and cool in the broth. Transfer the eggs and broth to an airtight container, and store in the refrigerator for up to 5 days.

SERVING TIP: These eggs are great as a side dish for breakfast or a snack on the go.

PICKLED MIXED VEGETABLES

Pào Cài 泡菜

FAMILY: LI YUNZHOU 李运洲 AND ZHOU YI 周熠 | SHIMEN, HUNAN

This simple dish opens the appetite for the next courses. Serve it at the beginning of the meal, and keep it on the table throughout.

2 medium carrots

1 medium daikon radish

1 medium cucumber

2 (1-inch) pieces fresh ginger, peeled, plus 5 (1-inch) pieces ginger, smacked

2 cloves garlic

1 teaspoon Sichuan peppercorns

6 fresh red chiles

3 tablespoons rice wine vinegar or apple cider vinegar

1 tablespoon sugar

1 tablespoon sea salt

2 sprigs cilantro, roughly chopped, for garnish

Slice the carrot, daikon, cucumber, garlic, and the 2 pieces of peeled ginger into thin diagonal slices. (Use a mandoline if you have one; it will save you time.) Cut the garlic cloves into thumbnail slices. Place the vegetables in a large heatproof glass bowl.

In a wok over high heat, boil 2 cups of water. Add the peppercorns, the 5 pieces of smacked ginger, and red chiles, and boil for 3 minutes. Remove from the heat and stir in the vinegar, sugar, and salt until the sugar and salt dissolve. Let cool, then pour over the vegetables. Cover and chill in the refrigerator overnight. You can now keep the pickled vegetables in an airtight container in the refrigerator for up to a month.

Garnish with the cilantro before serving.

VARIATION TIP: Add 1 tablespoon of Scorched Chili Oil (page 37) for a touch of nutty roasted chili flavor.

STEAMED RICE PEARLS WITH PORK

Zhēn Zhū Wán Zi 珍珠丸子

FAMILY: XU WEIWEN 许伟文 | WUXI, JIANGSU

Don't be fooled by the title—this is more of a meatball than a rice pearl. Xu Weiwen, the father who taught me how to make this treat, made every dish look easy to prepare. And it is, with a little advance preparation. This simple crowd pleaser can be served as an appetizer or side dish at a dinner party.

Special equipment:
2 bamboo steamer baskets, and parchment paper or napa cabbage leaves to line the baskets

½ cup uncooked glutinous rice

½ pound fatty ground pork

2 tablespoons dried shiitake mushrooms, minced

2 tablespoons wood ear mushrooms, minced

2 tablespoons fresh bamboo shoots, minced

1 tablespoon Shaoxing cooking wine or dry sherry

1 tablespoon chicken stock

1 large egg, beaten

1 teaspoon peeled fresh ginger, minced

1 teaspoon potato starch

1 teaspoon sea salt

½ teaspoon freshly ground white pepper

In a medium bowl, add the uncooked glutinous rice and cover with cold water. Set aside to soak for at least 2 hours or overnight, if possible.

In a large mixing bowl, combine the pork, shiitake mushrooms, wood ear mushrooms, bamboo shoots, wine, stock, egg, ginger, potato starch, salt, and pepper. Set aside.

Drain the rice in a fine-mesh sieve and tap the edge to remove excess water. Spread the rice on a plate.

Add water to the wok to a level just below the bottom of the lower steamer basket. Line the baskets with parchment paper or a large napa cabbage leaf to prevent food from sticking to the basket. Bring the water to a rapid boil over high heat, then lower to medium-high heat.

Roll 2 teaspoons of the pork mixture filling into meatballs the size of Ping-Pong balls. Roll each ball in the glutinous rice, coating the entire surface.

Place the balls in the steamer baskets with a bit of space between them, and steam for 20 to 22 minutes. The rice will look translucent, and the pork beneath will lend a pinkish hue.

SERVING TIP: Serve with soy sauce and chili oil. Guests can mix the soy sauce and chili oil to their own preference for a dipping sauce.

INGREDIENT TIP: Glutinous rice is gluten-free; the term 'glutinous' refers to its glue-like stickiness. It is widely available.

COLD SMACKED RADISHES

Liáng Bàn Yáng Huā Luó Bo 凉拌扬花萝卜

FAMILY: LU GUANGRONG 路广荣 | NANJING, JIANGSU

Although the large white radish known as daikon is native to China, the more commonly known red radish is not. Nonetheless, there is a traditional tale that roots it in China—specifically Nanjing, where I learned this recipe. The story says that long ago, there was a young radish farmer called Yang Hua from Nanjing. One year, the radish tops were a brilliant green, so Yang Hua assumed the radishes were enormous. The farmer was disappointed when he pulled them out and found that they were no larger than the size of his big toe. Out of curiosity he tasted one, and to his surprise discovered it was crisp and deliciously spicy. He sold them on the street, and people flocked to his stall for more. The cherry-colored vegetable would become known in China as *Yang Hua* radish.

2 bunches small red radishes

1 teaspoon sea salt

1 tablespoon soy sauce

1 tablespoon rice wine vinegar

1 teaspoon sesame oil

1 teaspoon caster or superfine sugar
(see Ingredient Tip)

Wash and trim the radishes. On the cutting board, smack each radish with the flat side of your cleaver—the goal is "smack 'em to crack 'em." Put in a medium bowl and add the salt. Mix well, and set aside for 20 minutes. The salt will draw out water from the radishes.

In a small bowl, combine the soy sauce, vinegar, oil, and sugar. Set aside.

Just before serving, drain the radishes. Tap the strainer to remove excess liquid.

Transfer the radishes to a small serving bowl. Pour the sauce over the radishes, toss, and serve.

INGREDIENT TIP: If you don't have caster sugar, you can process granulated sugar in a blender in ½-cup increments. Pulse three times or until the sugar is superfine.

SMACKED CUCUMBER SALAD

Liáng Bàn Huáng Guā 凉拌黄瓜

FAMILY: ZHANG XINYU 张欣雨 | CHENGDU, SICHUAN

"Smacking" is one of my favorite cooking techniques, perhaps because it is so immediate and familiar. There's no dancing around to find a graceful way to do something that just requires simple honesty: Smack the garlic to better mince it. Smack the cucumber so it absorbs more of the dressing's flavor.

1 (8-inch) cucumber, smacked and sliced

9 cloves garlic, smacked and minced

5 teaspoons sesame oil

2 teaspoons sea salt

1 teaspoon white vinegar

5 drops freshly squeezed lemon juice

Put the cucumber and garlic in a medium bowl. Add the sesame oil, salt, and vinegar, and mix together.

Sprinkle the lemon juice over the cucumber salad.

VARIATION TIP: Use a mixture of raw daikon and cucumber for variety. Or add a tablespoon of Scorched Chili Oil (page 37) for some heat.

SCRAMBLED EGG WITH TOMATO

Xī Hóng Shì Chǎo Jī Dàn 西红柿炒鸡蛋

FAMILY: HAN XIANMING 韩先明 | TONGZHOU, BEIJING

This simple dish is ubiquitous in China. I rarely cook scrambled eggs now without tomato and garlic—it takes me back to my travels.

1 tablespoon peanut oil, divided

1 small clove garlic, minced

1 ripe tomato, roughly chopped

3 eggs, beaten

Pinch sea salt

1 scallion, green part, finely chopped

Heat ½ tablespoon of peanut oil in a wok over high heat. Add the garlic and stir-fry until fragrant, about 10 seconds. Add the tomato and stir-fry until the skin starts to loosen from the flesh. Remove the tomato from the wok and set aside in a small bowl.

Heat the remaining ½ tablespoon of peanut oil in the wok over medium heat. Add the eggs and the salt, and scramble until half-way cooked, then return the tomato to the wok and stir-fry until the eggs are cooked to your preference.

Transfer the eggs to a plate and garnish with the scallion greens.

SERVING TIP: You can serve this dish by itself or over rice. I like to warm up already cooked rice in the rice cooker, and serve the eggs and tomato atop a bowl of rice. Also, save the unused white part of the scallion in the refrigerator for another use in another meal or freeze it to put in stock later.

THOUSAND-YEAR-OLD EGGS WITH DOUBLE CHILES

Shuāng Jiāo Pí Dàn 双椒皮蛋

FAMILY: ZHOU JUXIANG 周菊香 | CHANGSHA, HUNAN

Thousand-Year-Old eggs (preserved duck eggs) have a rich, creamy flavor. To truly enjoy this, it is helpful to be open to strong flavors. The chile dressing adds a depth of flavor to this dish, which sings with aged vinegar, nutty sesame oil, and garlic. These eggs can be found at most Asian grocery stores.

1 hot green chile, cut in half and seeded

1 sweet red chile, cut in half and seeded

1 clove garlic, minced

1 teaspoon sea salt

1 tablespoon Chinkiang vinegar or balsamic vinegar

1 tablespoon sesame oil

3 preserved duck eggs, peeled

Scorch the chiles in a dry wok, stirring, for 2 minutes over low heat, and set aside to cool.

Finely chop the chiles and put in a small bowl. Add the garlic, salt, vinegar, and sesame oil, and toss.

Slice the eggs lengthwise into 6 to 8 wedges, and arrange on a round plate. Drizzle the eggs with the chile dressing just before serving.

COOKING TIP: Peel the eggs submerged in cool water for easier peeling and to rinse away sediment.

VARIATION TIP: When serving, add 1 tablespoon of Scorched Chili Oil (page 37) with sediment for a toasty kick.

TWICE-COOKED EGGS

Huí Guō Jī Dàn 回锅鸡蛋

FAMILY: ZHOU YI 周熠 | SHIMEN, HUNAN

This dish might be the Chinese answer to deviled eggs, or not. Either way, it's a treat. Zhou Yi, the woman who taught me this dish, was a rosy-cheeked young woman with a big personality. I imagine she would have been the girl to protect me in the school yard and set everyone else straight. No one messed with Zhou Yi. But she wasn't a bully; she was more like everyone's mom. Her husband Li Yunzhou was quieter, but both were good humored about everything. They were eager to take me through their town market in Shimen, and then prepare all the dishes they typically served for a meal. Zhou Yi beamed with excitement as she demonstrated this one. I understood— eggs excite me, too! Especially ones topped with Scorched Chili Oil and scallions—just mouthwatering!

1 teaspoon sea salt

6 large eggs

2 teaspoons black (or any color) sesame seeds

2 tablespoons peanut oil

Scorched Chili Oil (page 37), with sediment

1 scallion, green part, finely chopped

SERVING TIP: Serve as a side dish for breakfast or lunch. It also makes a yummy appetizer before dinner.

SUBSTITUTION TIP: Black sesame seeds are preferable in this dish for the color contrast, but any color sesame seeds will do.

In a large bowl, create an ice water bath by placing ice cubes in cold water.

In a large saucepan, bring 6 cups of water to a boil with the salt. Carefully lower the eggs into the saucepan and boil for 6 minutes. Remove the pan from the heat, and transfer the eggs to the ice water bath to stop them from cooking. Once cool, peel the eggs and cut them in half lengthwise.

Heat the wok over high heat, then reduce the heat to low. Add the sesame seeds to the dry wok and slowly stir to toast. You should start to smell a nutty aroma. When the seeds start popping, remove them to a small dish.

Heat the peanut oil in the wok, and place the eggs curved side down in the wok, frying them over low heat until the bottoms are golden. Remove them with a slotted spoon and transfer to a plate.

Drizzle the eggs with the scorched chili oil and sediment, garnish with the scallions, and sprinkle with salt and the toasted sesame seeds.

PORK AND CABBAGE DUMPLINGS

Zhū Ròu Bái Cài Shuǐ Jiǎo 猪肉白菜水饺

FAMILY: HAN XIANMING 韩先明 | TONGZHOU, BEIJING

"How many dumplings can you eat?" Han Ayi asked with her eyes sparkling, ready to challenge my reply. "I can eat eight to ten dumplings," was my answer. "Really?!" she scoffed with cackling laughter before telling me she could eat 24 dumplings and her husband, several more. I could never eat that many dumplings in one sitting, but if there were any chance that I might, I would probably most enjoy stuffing myself with Han Ayi's dumplings. I believe it was how she seasoned the oil with Sichuan peppercorns before mixing it into the dumpling filling. Whether you're mixing a meat or vegetarian dumpling filling, season the oil with Sichuan peppercorns for a special flavor you might not find anywhere other than Beijing. Dumpling wrappers can either be homemade (page 42) or bought fresh from an Asian grocery store (get the round ones).

FOR THE SICHUAN PEPPERCORN-SEASONED OIL

1½ tablespoons peanut oil

2 teaspoons Sichuan peppercorns

FOR THE DUMPLINGS

11 ounces ground pork

5 ounces napa cabbage, finely chopped

1 tablespoon Shaoxing cooking wine or dry sherry

1 tablespoon dark soy sauce

1 teaspoon soy sauce

2 scallions, green and white parts, finely chopped

1 teaspoon sesame oil

1 tablespoon Sichuan peppercorn–seasoned oil

½ teaspoon sugar

2 tablespoons chicken stock

1 teaspoon sea salt

30 to 40 dumpling wrappers

1 tablespoon peanut oil

TO MAKE THE SICHUAN PEPPERCORN–SEASONED OIL

In a wok over medium-high heat, heat the 1½ tablespoons of peanut oil. When hot, add the Sichuan peppercorns and stir-fry for 1 to 2 minutes. Remove from the heat.

Using a slotted spoon, remove the peppercorns and discard. Reserve the oil in a heat-proof container for the filling.

TO MAKE THE DUMPLINGS

In a large mixing bowl, combine the pork, cabbage, cooking wine, dark soy sauce, soy sauce, scallions, sesame oil, peppercorn-seasoned oil, sugar, stock, and salt. Hold a dumpling wrapper in the palm of one hand. Put 1 heaping teaspoon of filling into the center of the wrapper, then fold in half. With one finger, moisten the edges of the wrapper with water, and then pinch and pleat the edges to seal. Transfer the dumpling to a flour-dusted plate. Wrap and seal the remaining dumplings.

Add the remaining 1 tablespoon of peanut oil to a large pot of water over high heat. Bring the water to a rolling boil. Cook the dumplings in batches so as not to crowd the pot, adding 8 to 10 dumplings at a time to the boiling water. When the water starts to foam and rise, add 1 cup of cold water. This helps the water cool down so the filling can cook thoroughly. When the water rises again, add another cup of cold water. Continue cooking until the water rises again, then remove the dumplings. Repeat with the remaining dumplings. Serve hot.

SERVING SUGGESTION: Serve the dumplings with a sauce made of Chinkiang vinegar or balsamic vinegar, Scorched Chili Oil (page 37), and soy sauce. The ratio is entirely up to you, but northern-style dumplings are typically dipped or drenched in vinegar.

LEFTOVERS TIP: You may not be able to eat as many dumplings as Han Ayi and her husband can. Wrap leftover dumplings in plastic wrap and refrigerate for up to 3 days. To reheat, pan-fry in 2 tablespoons of peanut oil.

EGG DUMPLINGS

Dàn Jiǎo 蛋饺

FAMILY: ZHU DANDAN 朱丹丹 | BEIJING

This dish could be your dinner party trick, so you might want to wait until your friends arrive to make them. They'll be impressed with your culinary prowess! And then they can enjoy them hot, as well. Zhu Dandan used wild rice stems in the stir-fry portion of the dish. They're a lot like bamboo shoots—mild in flavor and crisp in texture. You can find these at Asian grocers like Ranch 99.

FOR THE DUMPLINGS

8 ounces ground pork

½ teaspoon sea salt

1 tablespoon dark soy sauce

8 large or 10 medium eggs, beaten

Peanut oil

FOR THE STIR-FRY

4 ounces wild rice stems, fresh diced bamboo shoots, or diced asparagus

4 ounces Chinese yam or potato, diced

4 ounces carrots, diced

4 ounces fresh shiitake or crimini mushrooms, diced

2 cloves garlic, minced

2 tablespoons peanut oil

1 medium cucumber, diced

Egg dumplings (see above)

2 teaspoons sea salt, divided

1 tablespoon dark soy sauce

TO MAKE THE DUMPLINGS

Combine the pork, salt, and soy sauce. Add enough water to create a soft, thick, batterlike consistency. Let sit for 5 minutes to blend.

In a mixing bowl, beat the eggs.

In a wok heated over high heat, add the oil to ¼ inch deep and heat. Pour in 1 tablespoon of beaten egg, creating a small pancake. This is the dumpling wrapper. (Beware, it may sputter.) When the egg flowers with bubbles, add a teaspoon-size ball of pork filling to the center. Using a pair of chopsticks and a spatula, bring one edge of the egg wrapper to the other edge, creating a half-moon shape, like a mini omelet. Flip the dumpling to cook both sides until golden, and remove to a plate. The dumpling filling will not be completely cooked. Repeat with the remaining dumpling filling and eggs.

MAKE THE DUMPLING STIR-FRY

In a medium pot filled with water over high heat, parboil the wild rice stems, Chinese yam, carrots, and mushrooms for 5 minutes. With a slotted spoon, remove the vegetables to a plate.

In a wok, heat the peanut oil over medium-high heat until it shimmers. Add the garlic and stir-fry until fragrant, about 10 seconds. Add the reserved wild rice stems, Chinese yam, carrots, and mushrooms, and stir-fry for 4 minutes. Add the cucumber, salt, and dark soy sauce, and stir-fry for 2 minutes.

Add the egg dumplings to the wok, and gently toss them with the vegetables, taking care not to break the dumplings. Stir-fry for 1 minute to reheat the dumplings.

Transfer the stir-fry to a large serving dish and serve.

SERVING SUGGESTION: The vegetable stir-fry makes a perfect meal.

VARIATION TIP: You can omit the vegetables and serve the egg dumplings by themselves with just a dipping sauce combining Scorched Chili Oil (page 37) and soy sauce.

HAKKA-STYLE STUFFED TOFU

Kè Jiā Niàng Dòu Fu 客家酿豆腐

FAMILY: QIU HE 邱河 | MEIXIAN, GUANGDONG

This dish is an example of Hakka cuisine (see page 63). As Wen Po taught me, making stuffed tofu is not a process to be rushed. Take your time, and fill the tofu pieces carefully so they don't split open.

FOR THE STUFFED TOFU

1 pound ground pork

4 ounces dried squid or dried shrimp, minced (see Substitution Tip)

3 scallions, finely chopped

1 shallot, finely chopped

3 teaspoons potato starch

1 teaspoon sea salt

½ teaspoon ground white pepper

1 egg white

3 (14-ounce) boxes firm tofu, cut into triangular wedges

2 tablespoons peanut oil

FOR THE STIR-FRY

1 tablespoon peanut oil

1 large tomato, sliced into wedges

1 scallion, green and white parts, cut into 1-inch pieces

2 tablespoons soy sauce

½ teaspoon freshly ground white pepper

1 teaspoon potato starch

Sea salt

TO MAKE THE STUFFED TOFU

In a large mixing bowl, add the pork, dried squid, scallions, shallot, potato starch, salt, pepper, and egg white. Stir together to blend well. Cover the dish with plastic wrap and refrigerate.

Cut one brick of tofu diagonally to form two triangles. Cut both triangles in half. Repeat this for the remaining two tofu bricks. Slice into the long edge of the tofu wedge, scooping out a little to form a pocket.

Remove the pork filling from the refrigerator. Take a teaspoon—or try your talent with chopsticks—and carefully stuff the tofu pocket with some of the filling. Press the filling securely but gently into the pocket; the tofu wedge will bulge a bit. Repeat for the remaining pieces.

In a wok, heat the peanut oil over high heat until shimmering. Carefully place 4 stuffed tofu wedges in the wok, and fry until golden, about 2 minutes each side. Fry the tofu wedges in batches so you don't overcrowd the pan. With a slotted spoon or spider, transfer the cooked tofu to a serving plate.

TO MAKE THE STIR-FRY

Heat the peanut oil in the wok over high heat until shimmering. Add the tomato, scallion, soy sauce, and pepper. Stir-fry for 1 minute.

Meanwhile, in a small bowl, combine the potato starch and 2 tablespoons of water, stirring to mix well. Add to the wok, and stir-fry until the sauce is completely mixed. Season with salt. Pour the sauce over the stuffed tofu wedges.

COOKING TIP: The more finely you chop the filling ingredients, the easier it will be to stuff the tofu. Using chopsticks really helps stuff the filling more delicately than with a spoon—and it adds authenticity to your efforts!

SUBSTITUTION TIP: Dried shrimp is widely available at Asian grocers. Ingredients like dried shrimp or dried shiitake mushrooms are used to add umami to a dish. But if you wish, fresh shrimp can also be used. Mixing pork with shrimp or fish brings out even more umami in a dish. The blend of meat and seafood tastes much richer than using just one or the other.

LOTUS ROOT WITH GINGER DRESSING

Jiāng Zhī Ǒu Piàn 姜汁藕片

FAMILY: DANG QIN 党琴 | QINGDAO, SHANDONG

There's something so satisfying about biting into crisp lotus root. It's a little like jicama or fresh water chestnut, and available at many Asian markets. I learned this recipe from a family in Qingdao, where seafood is famously fresh. And, incidentally, so is Tsingtao beer, which can be bought by the liter in this seaside town where it's originally from. I think this cold dish adds freshness to a meal of seafood and beer. This recipe uses not only the leaves of cilantro, but also the flavorful stems.

½ teaspoon sea salt

½ pound fresh lotus root, cut into ¼-inch-thick slices

1 teaspoon caster sugar (or superfine granulated sugar)

2 teaspoons rice wine vinegar

5 sprigs cilantro (leaves and stems), minced

1 (1-inch) piece peeled fresh ginger, minced

1 teaspoon sesame oil

Bring 3 cups of water and salt to boil in a wok over high heat. Add the sliced lotus root and parboil for 2 minutes. Drain and rinse in cold water. Transfer to a plate.

In a large bowl, stir together the sugar, vinegar, cilantro, ginger, and sesame oil.

Add the lotus root and toss gently to coat with the dressing. Serve on a plate, arranged to display the pretty lacelike pattern of the lotus slices.

SERVING TIP: For extra crispness, chill in the refrigerator for about 1 hour.

MEETING ROSE'S AUNT

I am fascinated by the Chinese diaspora. I traveled to Meixian and met a family of the Hakka minority group. Hakka people migrated from China to Indonesia, and descendants dispersed from there; some moved to the United States, while others, like my 82-year-old host, Qiu He—affectionately called Wen Po—"returned" to China. Wen Po referred to herself as *huaqiao*, someone who has lived abroad. Of her family, she alone returned to China while much of her family stayed abroad.

My former colleague at eBay, Rose, had seen me post about my search for Chinese family recipes in China. She told me of the great-aunt she had never met, known in the family for her Hakka home cooking. I love Hakka cuisine, and naturally, the relationship between Rose in the US and her great-aunt in China intrigued me.

When I arrived at Wen Po's home, she approached me warmly, clutching my arms and welcoming us with a grandmotherly voice. She showed me a photograph of herself seated with her siblings 20 years earlier. After a bit of discussion, we figured out which sibling's daughter I knew.

Wen Po had trouble moving about, so her neighbor, Fan Shifu, cooked while Wen Po directed. I learned how to make steamed pork belly with preserved mustard greens, sweet and sour fish, and Hakka-Style Stuffed Tofu (page 60).

Wen Po's son and Rose's cousin, Wen Li, came home for lunch, dressed in his police officer's uniform. He warmed a pot of the local *nuomi jiu* (glutinous rice wine). It was sweet and too easy to drink with the well-salted food!

After the meal, we sat in the living room, enjoying multiple cups of tea and slices of pomelo (a large Asian citrus fruit). Wen Li sent us off with two pomelos and two gallons of wine. When visiting families, I would often ask myself why I was so lucky to meet such wonderful people and experience such warmth paired with food. After this visit, I wished my colleague could have joined me in this full circle of connection with relatives that she had never met. I'm grateful Rose suggested the visit, and I hope it is something she can add to her family stories.

The meal's cook, Fan Jiawei; family friend Li Suping; Wen Po's daughter-in-law, Chen Ying; Wen Po; Wen Po's son, Wen Li.

EIGHT-TREASURE SPICY SAUCE

Bā Bǎo Là Jiàng 八宝辣酱

FAMILY: GONG DONGHUA 龚冬华 | SHANGHAI

This famous dish is a classic of Shanghai cuisine. Chen Chen was a young college-age man who gave swimming lessons to one of my friend's children. He lived with his family in new apartments in the Pudong district of Shanghai. Though their home was newer than most homes I'd visited—lots of sunlight and clean, modern furniture— the kitchen was still a modest size. One thing that never ceased to amaze me was how much food could be cooked for so many guests in these small kitchens. Chen Chen's family was warm, welcoming, and like most Chinese families, very hospitable. His mother taught me how to make traditional Shanghai dishes and served this dish with other local specialties in a feast. Keep this one in mind for when you decide to host a dinner party and need a dreamy sauce to top chewy noodles.

FOR THE SHRIMP BATTER

⅓ cup shelled fresh peas

5 shrimp, peeled and deveined, finely chopped

2 teaspoons Shaoxing cooking wine or dry sherry

½ teaspoon potato starch

1 egg white, beaten

¼ teaspoon sea salt

FOR THE SAUCE

6 tablespoons peanut oil, divided

1 cup raw peanuts, without skins

4 tablespoons miso paste

2 tablespoons sweet noodle sauce

2 teaspoons minced peeled fresh ginger

1 teaspoon minced garlic

2 ounces smoked tofu (baked teriyaki-flavored tofu is also fine), cut into ¼ inch by ¼ inch cubes

3 ounces bamboo shoots, finely chopped

4 ounces ground lean pork

22 ginkgo nuts, peeled (peeled edamame can be substituted)

½ medium carrot, finely chopped

1 teaspoon sugar

TO MAKE THE SHRIMP BATTER

In a small bowl, combine the peas, shrimp, cooking wine, potato starch, and egg white. Set aside.

TO MAKE THE SAUCE

Heat 4 tablespoons of peanut oil in a wok over medium heat until the oil shimmers. Add the peanuts and stir-fry continuously until golden, about 6 minutes. Reduce the heat if you notice the peanuts getting too brown. Using a slotted spoon, remove the peanuts to a plate and set aside. Reheat the oil in the wok to medium heat.

While continually stir-frying, add the miso paste, bean paste, ginger, and garlic, and stir-fry until you have a well-combined sauce. Add the smoked tofu, bamboo shoots, pork, ginkgo nuts, and carrot. Add the sugar and 1 tablespoon of water (the moisture helps cook the ingredients). Cover and simmer for 3 minutes. Return the peanuts to the wok and stir-fry for 2 minutes. Transfer the sauce to a serving bowl. Rinse the wok and return it to the stove.

In the wok over medium heat, add the remaining 2 tablespoons of peanut oil and heat until shimmering. Add the reserved shrimp batter and continue to stir-fry until the egg white has firmed. Add the salt and mix well. Transfer to the bowl with the sauce and mix well.

SERVING TIP: This hearty meat sauce is typically served over Steamed Rice (page 36). It's the perfect comfort dish. I've also found it to be perfect over Hand-made Noodles (page 43). Given its auspicious eight ingredients (the number eight is lucky in Chinese culture), I've served it over noodles for a birthday party to maximize the symbolism of luck and longevity contained in the meal. Noodles are typically eaten for a birthday because just as the noodle is long and should never be cut, life is wished to be a long and happy one.

COOKING TIP: Medium heat is best for cooking raw peanuts. If the heat is too high, the surface of the peanuts will burn before the inside has cooked.

SOUPS & SALADS

Wonton Chicken Soup (page 70)

CORN AND PORK RIBS SOUP

Pái Gǔ Yù Mǐ Tāng 排骨玉米汤

FAMILY: ZHOU JUXIANG 周菊香 | CHANGSHA, HUNAN

This soup is as simple and down to earth as the family who introduced me to it. When I arrived at the bus stop in Changsha, Zhou Ayi met my friend Juling and me with a light sea-green umbrella. It drizzled as we followed her to her apartment along a path that wove between piles of rubble. Zhou Ayi explained that she was among several residents in the area holding onto their homes, refusing to vacate to make room for expensive high rises. The push was forcing residents to relocate outside the city limits in search of affordable housing. I sympathized with Zhou Ayi and her family. I was familiar with their plight; this was happening in other areas of China, and around the world. So my visit to Zhou Ayi's home is one that is dear to me, as I remember the family's pride and the simple yet tasty food she shared. YIELD: SERVES 6 TO 8

1 ¾ pounds pork spareribs, chopped into 1 ½-inch cubes

3 ears corn, cut into 1- to 2-inch pieces

1 carrot, cut into 1-inch pieces

1 cup chicken stock

1 tablespoon soy sauce

2 teaspoons sea salt

1 scallion, green part, finely chopped

In a large pot over high heat, bring 6 cups of water to a boil. Parboil the pork spareribs for 10 minutes, then drain and rinse.

Return the ribs to the pot and add 6 cups of water. Over high heat, bring to a boil, then add the corn, carrot, stock, soy sauce, and salt. Reduce the heat to medium, and simmer for 1 hour.

Garnish with the scallion and serve.

COOKING TIP: You can use a pressure cooker to cook this soup in just 20 minutes.

JADE SOUP

Fĕi Cuì Tāng 翡翠汤

FAMILY: XIAO XIA 肖霞 | CHENGDU, SICHUAN

Xiao Ayi is a mother whose rosy cheeks glow. My first impression of the Luo family was one of awe, both because of the mother's care toward feeding her family, and because of how well mannered and engaging her sons were. Xiao Ayi puréed fresh winter amaranth (a once-wild, nutritious, protein-rich annual green), then simmered it with chicken bone stock. Just before serving, she dropped heavy cream into the jade pool, her eyes hypnotized by the clouds of cream blooming in the velvety soup. Xiao Ayi transformed the winter amaranth into soup form because her children are still getting used to eating vegetables. You see, they won't eat "vegetables," but they'll eat this beautiful soup. Smart mom! YIELD: SERVES 6 TO 8

4 to 5 ounces winter amaranth, or spinach

3 cups chicken stock, divided

1 teaspoon sea salt

1 teaspoon soybean paste, or miso paste

¼ teaspoon potato starch

1 tablespoon heavy cream

Using a food processor or blender, purée the amaranth with ½ cup of stock.

In a large saucepan over medium-high heat, add the puréed amaranth, the remaining 2½ cups of stock, and the salt, and bring to a simmer, stirring occasionally.

Add the soybean paste, and simmer for 2 minutes.

In a small bowl, add ¾ cup of cold water and the potato starch, stir to dissolve, and add to the simmering soup. Simmer for 2 minutes.

Transfer to a serving bowl or individual small bowls, and garnish with a few drops of cream.

SERVING TIP: The cream is supposed to be optional, but Xiao Ayi added it, and it was a great complement.

WONTON CHICKEN SOUP

Ji Tāng Hún Tún 鸡汤馄饨

FAMILY: XU WEIWEN 许伟文 | WUXI, JIANGSU

Xu Shushu was often asked to cook for weddings, and this soup was always at the top of his banquet repertoire. The wonton dumplings represent old Chinese money, bringing luck and fortune to the newlyweds. I was introduced to Xu Shushu by his daughter Lijia, a sweet young woman whose kindness I soon noticed was just like her father's. It was easy to imagine Xu Shushu offering his skills to his friends and community when they needed someone to cook for their weddings. Weddings are special, but in China they were not always glamorous, especially under stricter Communist rule. During simpler times, people leaned on each other. Today, Wuxi is a bigger city and many weddings now require catering on a restaurant scale, but Xu Shushu is still sought after to cook—because he does it from the heart. YIELD: SERVES 10 TO 12

FOR THE WONTONS

1 pound ground pork

4 wood ear mushrooms, finely chopped

2 scallions, finely chopped

1 (1-inch) piece peeled fresh ginger, minced

2 cloves garlic, minced

1 egg white, beaten

2 teaspoons sesame oil

1 tablespoon potato starch

1 teaspoon sea salt

1 teaspoon freshly ground white pepper

1 recipe Dumpling Wrappers (page 42), or 1 package purchased round dumpling wrappers

Peanut oil, for frying

FOR THE SOUP

1½ quarts chicken stock

3 scallions, finely chopped, white and green parts, divided

1 (1-inch) piece peeled fresh ginger, smacked and thinly sliced

1 teaspoon sea salt

1 teaspoon freshly ground white pepper

Sesame oil, for garnish

TO MAKE THE WONTONS

In a large bowl, combine the pork, mushrooms, scallions, ginger, garlic, egg white, oil, potato starch, salt, and pepper. Mix thoroughly.

Into the center of one wonton wrapper, put 1 heaping teaspoon of filling. Fold the wrapper in half and press the edges together to seal. Then bring the two ends together and seal with a pinch. Repeat until all the filling and wrappers are used.

Add enough peanut oil to the wok to deep-fry the wontons, and heat over medium-high heat. When the oil is hot and shimmering, add 6 to 8 dumplings. Be sure not to crowd them—the more room they have, the better they'll fry. Fry until golden, about 4 minutes. With a slotted spoon, remove the wontons to a paper towel–lined plate to drain.

TO MAKE THE SOUP

In a large pot over high heat, bring the stock to a simmer. Add the scallion white parts, ginger, salt, and pepper. Simmer for 3 to 4 minutes. Reduce the heat to low, cover the pot, and keep hot until ready to serve.

To serve, use 10 to 12 small rice or soup bowls. Place 2 wonton dumplings in each bowl, then pour the hot soup over them. Garnish with the scallion green parts and a few drops of sesame oil.

COOKING TIP: If you're making your own dumpling wrappers, roll out each wrapper as thinly as possible for crisper wontons.

WINTER MELON SOUP

Dōng Guā Tāng 冬瓜湯

This light soup is a nice accompaniment to a Chinese meal. Low-calorie and a mild diuretic, it is a good soup if you're trying to shred a few pounds or detoxify your system. Winter melon can be found at Asian grocers and farmers' markets, but in a pinch, you can substitute daikon radish. YIELD: SERVES 6 TO 8

1 pound winter melon, or daikon radish

¼ cup fresh or dried wood ear mushrooms

6 cups chicken stock (page 40)

2 (1-inch) pieces peeled fresh ginger, sliced

1 teaspoon sea salt

1 tablespoon soy sauce

1 teaspoon freshly ground white pepper

1 teaspoon sesame oil

3 sprigs cilantro (leaves and stems), roughly chopped

Peel and seed the winter melon. Cut into 1-inch cubes and put in a medium bowl.

If using dried wood ear mushrooms, soak in warm water for 20 to 30 minutes to rehydrate, then rinse and drain. Tear into bite-size pieces.

In a large pot over medium heat, slowly bring the stock to a simmer. Add the winter melon, mushrooms, ginger, and salt. Simmer for 20 to 30 minutes, until the winter melon is translucent and soft. Stir in the soy sauce, pepper, and sesame oil. Serve hot, garnished with the cilantro.

VARIATION TIP: For a heartier dish, try adding Chinese cured ham or Chinese sausage. You can even add some dumplings during the last 15 minutes of simmering. This soup can also be garnished with chopped scallion.

HOT AND SOUR SOUP

Suān Là Tāng 酸辣湯

In the dry, below-freezing winters of Beijing, there were a number of ways to warm up: drink *baijiu* (Chinese rice liquor), eat *chao ganr* (an offal soup enjoyed by Beijing old-timers), or drink hot tea and hot and sour soup. My choice was often the latter. The key to good hot and sour soup is the balance between the Chinkiang vinegar and the other ingredients. I soon grew accustomed to Chinese vinegar with my dumplings and enjoyed it in this soup. Fend off the cold with my recipe for this familiar treat.

YIELD: SERVES 6 TO 8

1 cup dried shiitake mushrooms

¼ cup dried or fresh wood ear mushrooms

8 ounces firm tofu

6 cups chicken stock (page 40)

1 teaspoon sea salt, plus more for seasoning

2 eggs, beaten

2 teaspoons sesame oil, plus more if desired

1 tablespoon soy sauce

1 tablespoon dark soy sauce

⅓ cup Chinkiang vinegar, or balsamic vinegar

1 tablespoon Scorched Chili Oil (page 37), without sediment

Freshly ground white pepper

Cilantro, torn into short sprigs for garnish

Soak the dried shiitakes (and the wood ear mushrooms if using the dried variety) in a bowl of warm water for about 30 minutes or until soft and easy to slice. Drain, and trim any woody stems and tough bits. Cut the mushrooms into thin strips.

Cut the tofu into very thin slices—about the same as the mushroom strips.

In a wok over high heat, add the stock and bring to a boil. Reduce the heat and gently simmer. Stir in the salt, wood ear mushrooms, and shiitake mushrooms, and simmer for 2 minutes.

In a small bowl, combine the eggs and sesame oil. Slowly drizzle the egg mixture into the soup, while using a spoon to gently separate the egg into thin, small sheets.

Remove the soup from the heat, and stir in the soy sauce, dark soy sauce, vinegar, and Scorched Chili Oil. Season with salt, pepper, and sesame oil.

Serve garnished with the cilantro.

SERVING SUGGESTION: Serve this dish with sesame oil, vinegar, and Scorched Chili Oil (page 37) on the side so guests can adjust the soup to their taste. I've learned that in China, some people really like their vinegar and use a lot of it, while others don't. The amount specified in this recipe is a good starting point for most palates.

CELERY, PORK, AND TOFU SOUP

Qín Cài Chǎo Ròu Dùn Dòu Fǔ 芹菜炒肉炖豆腐

FAMILY: ZHOU YI 周熠 | SHIMEN, HUNAN

Zhou Yi, being the fun and creative person that she is, decorates her love nest with bright colors and works through conflicts with her husband by using Post-It notes—so it's fitting that she created this wonderful soup. Before she married, she worked and lived in various cities with roommates who enjoyed eating together. She and her roommates would cook up a wok full of this soup and have soup-eating contests to see who could eat the most bowls. YIELD: SERVES 4 TO 6

FOR THE PORK AND VEGETABLES

6 ounces pork tenderloin, chilled in the freezer for 15 minutes

2 cloves garlic, minced

1 (1-inch) piece peeled fresh ginger, minced

½ teaspoon potato starch

1½ teaspoons dark soy sauce

1 tablespoon Shaoxing cooking wine, or dry sherry

½ teaspoon sea salt

1 teaspoon chili powder

FOR THE SOUP

2 tablespoons peanut oil

1 teaspoon Sichuan peppercorns

6 stalks celery

1 (14-ounce) box tofu

1 teaspoon sea salt

TO MAKE THE PORK AND VEGETABLES

Cut the pork into 1-inch pieces, ¼ inch thick (thinner if possible).

In a medium bowl, combine the garlic, ginger, potato starch, dark soy sauce, cooking wine, salt, and chili powder. Add the pork strips and toss to coat. Set aside to marinate.

Remove the threads from the celery. Cut the celery into slices at a sharp diagonal angle (as thin as your pork slices). Cut the tofu in strips the same width as the celery.

TO MAKE THE SOUP

In a wok over high heat, heat the peanut oil until it is shimmering. Add the peppercorns and stir-fry until fragrant, about 10 seconds, then add the marinated pork and continue to stir-fry until the pork starts to brown, about 5 minutes. Add the celery and stir-fry for 1 minute. Add the tofu and stir-fry for 2 minutes.

Add the salt and 3 cups of water. Bring to a boil, reduce the heat to low, and simmer for 8 minutes. Transfer to a serving bowl, or serve immediately in small bowls.

COOKING TIP: You can make cutting meat easier by firming it up in the freezer for 15 to 30 minutes.

CHRYSANTHEMUM LEAF SOUP

Jú Huā Nǎo Yā Dàn Tāng 菊花脑鸭蛋汤

FAMILY: LU GUANGRONG 路广荣	NANJING, JIANGSU

A specialty of Nanjing, this famous, quick, and easy soup requires just a few ingredients and not much time. In Chinese traditional medicine, chrysanthemum leaves are used to cool the blood and lower blood pressure. YIELD: SERVES 4 TO 6

1 tablespoon sesame oil

2 cups chrysanthemum leaves, or arugula or spinach leaves

1 fresh duck egg
or 1 to 2 chicken eggs, beaten

1½ teaspoons sea salt

½ teaspoon freshly ground white pepper

In a wok over high heat, bring 3 cups of water to a boil, then reduce the heat to medium. Add the sesame oil and chrysanthemum leaves, tossing a little to submerge in the water. Add the egg, and continue to stir. Add the salt and pepper and simmer for 1 minute.

Remove from the heat and serve immediately.

SERVING TIP: People usually serve this dish in late spring and summer because of its cooling properties.

SUBSTITUION TIP: Arugula or spinach can be substituted for the chrysanthemum leaves. No matter which green you choose, however, take care to not overcook them as they can become slimy.

PORK AND DAIKON SOUP

Pái Gǔ Lúo Bo Tāng 排骨萝卜汤

FAMILY: ZHANG XINYU 张欣雨 | CHENGDU, SICHUAN

There's something about a tasty pork-bone broth that settles my being, or perhaps it's the familiar flavor I grew up with that connects me to this simple soup. It's a common soup in many Chinese households, but this particular recipe reminds me of one my mother used to make. Ask your butcher to cut up the pork ribs for you.

YIELD: SERVES 6 TO 8

1 pound pork ribs, cut into 1- to 2-inch pieces

1 (1-inch) piece peeled fresh ginger, thinly sliced

1 pound daikon radish

1½ teaspoon sea salt

½ teaspoon freshly ground white pepper

4 sprigs cilantro, roughly chopped

In a large pot over high heat, put in the pork ribs, ginger, and enough water to cover the ribs. Cover the pot and bring to a boil. Boil for 5 minutes, remove from heat, and drain the water. Rinse the pork of any sediment.

Return the pork and ginger to the pot and add 1½ quarts of water. Bring to a boil, reduce the heat to low, and simmer.

While the meat simmers, peel the daikon radish and cut into 1-inch cubes.

Add the daikon, salt, and pepper to the pork and continuing to simmer for 50 to 60 minutes, until pork and daikon are fork-tender.

Serve hot, garnished with the cilantro.

SERVING TIP: You can also garnish this dish with chopped scallion. For more texture, add a few torn pieces of wood ear mushroom.

FERN ROOT NOODLE SALAD

Jué Gēn Fěn 蕨根粉

FAMILY: HAN XIANMING 韩先明 | TONGZHOU, BEIJING

While living in China, I came to truly enjoy the many meat-free dishes available—especially this one. The cold noodles are lovely as a main dish on a warm summer day, and can also serve as a healthy meal starter year-round. Han Ayi taught me this simple recipe in her home in Tongzhou. The dish remains one of my all-time favorites. The vegetables offer crunch, and the noodles are slippery-delicious with the singing flavors of garlic, cilantro, chili oil, and sesame oil. Fern root noodles are made from the pulp of ferns from Sichuan. They can be found in the States in Asian supermarkets like Ranch 99.

1 cup shredded red cabbage

8 ounces dried fern root noodles

1 cucumber, julienned

1 carrot, julienned

3 sprigs cilantro (leaves and stems), roughly chopped

1 clove garlic, minced

2 tablespoons Scorched Chili Oil with sediment (page 37)

1 tablespoon oyster sauce

2 teaspoons Chinkiang vinegar, or balsamic vinegar

1 teaspoon soy sauce

1 teaspoon sesame oil

Sea salt

Blanch the red cabbage by parboiling for 2 minutes, then submerging in ice water to stop the cooking. Drain.

Bring a large pot of water to boil. Add the noodles and cook until tender, about 8 minutes. Pour into a colander, rinse with cold water, and drain. Transfer the noodles to a large bowl.

Add the cucumber, carrot, red cabbage, cilantro, garlic, chili oil, oyster sauce, vinegar, soy sauce, sesame oil, and season with salt. Add the noodles and toss to mix thoroughly.

COOKING TIP: Use a large pot to cook noodles, and stir them often to help them cook thoroughly and not stick together.

MINCED *KALIMERIS INDICA* WITH SMOKED TOFU

Mǎ Lán Bàn Xiāng Gān 马兰拌香干

FAMILY: XU WEIWEN 许伟文 | WUXI, JIANGSU

This salad is a lovely way to open up the appetite for your guests. *Kalimeris indica* is the botanical name for Indian aster, a wild green that grows in Southeast Asia. In that region, it is widely consumed as a nutritious vegetable with a distinctive flavor. It is also used in Chinese herbal medicine, and is hailed for its cooling and detoxifying qualities. I've read that *Kalimeris indica* has made its way into California, but it may still be difficult to find, so feel free to substitute spinach as the green in this dish. There are many kinds of smoked tofu to choose from in supermarkets. My favorite is an organic tofu braised in soy sauce, star anise, and cassia bark. It's made by Hodo and found at Whole Foods. For this dish, a few slices of the slab will impart a savory yet earthy flavor to the mild-tasting greens.

14 ounces *Kalimeris indica,* or spinach

3 (3- by 4-inch) thin slices smoked tofu

2 tablespoons sesame oil

1 teaspoon sea salt

¼ teaspoon sugar

Bring a medium pot of water to a boil over medium-high heat. Add the ***Kalimeris indica*** and boil gently for 2 to 3 minutes, until just tender. Greens are delicate, so watch carefully so you don't overcook them. Strain in a fine-mesh sieve, reserving the liquid. Pour the liquid back into the pot. Squeeze out any excess water from the greens and transfer to a cutting board. Chop finely and transfer to a large bowl.

With the pot over medium-high heat, bring the greens liquid to a boil. Add the tofu and parboil for 2 minutes. Remove from heat. Drain the tofu with a sieve and discard the water.

Cut the smoked tofu into strips, then chop ithe strips finely into ⅛-inch squares. Add the tofu to the bowl of greens. Add the oil, salt, and sugar, and toss gently to mix thoroughly.

Chill in the refrigerator for at least 1 hour. Serve cold.

SERVING TIP: Pack the prepared dish into a small bowl that can serve as a mold. Just before serving, turn the bowl over onto a plate and present this decorative variation.

WATERMELON RADISH SALAD

Liáng Bàn Xīn Líng Měi 凉拌心灵美

Watermelon radish is a beautiful vegetable and a festive addition to any meal. Just like red radishes, it is crisp, full of water, and has a peppery bite. For this dish, I recommend that you find a small watermelon radish, so you can slice perfect circles and retain the decorative white-to-pink pattern. This vegetable can be found at Whole Foods and farmers' markets, but regular radishes can be substituted.

1 small watermelon radish, or 1 bunch regular radishes

1 tablespoon rice vinegar

1 teaspoon sesame oil

¼ teaspoon sea salt

3 sprigs cilantro, roughly chopped, for garnish

Use a vegetable peeler to peel the tough outer skin off the watermelon radish.

Using a mandoline or a very sharp knife, thinly slice the radish crosswise to show the colorful pattern inside. Transfer the slices to a large bowl.

In a small bowl, combine the rice vinegar, sesame oil, and salt.

Pour the dressing over the radish slices and toss to coat.
To serve, garnish with the cilantro.

SERVING TIP: Serve this dish on a plate to show the radish's color and pattern. If you aren't able to find a small watermelon radish, you can cut a large radish into four wedges and cut those into triangle-shape watermelon slices. It's also pretty that way.

POULTRY

Kung Pao Chicken (page 90)

CHICKEN HOT POT

Tǔ Jī Huǒ Guō 土鸡火锅

FAMILY: MA HONG YU 马洪玉 | PUJI ZHEN, ZHANGQIU, SHANDONG

Most of the families who taught me how to make chicken stew or soup used what they called *tu ji*, or free-range chicken—they liked it best. Chinese families also tend to keep the bones in as the chicken cooks for flavoring, but you can bone the chicken before cooking if you prefer. This dish is an aromatic chicken stew braised in soy sauce and fragrant Chinese herbs. The family that taught me this dish transferred the cooked chicken to a copper hot pot bowl (a communal way to eat by cooking meat and vegetables in a shared bowl of broth simmering over a flame in the center of the table) fueled with charcoal to keep the dish simmering. The father continued to add water to the bowl as we ate dinner and we'd help ourselves to the broth. It isn't necessary to serve this dish in this pot, but it made for a festive presentation.

---

1 (3½ pound) chicken, cut into 1- to 2-inch pieces

2 tablespoons peanut oil

2 (1-inch) pieces peeled fresh ginger, sliced diagonally

4 (1-inch) pieces cassia bark or cinnamon bark

3 pods black cardamom or 2 white pods and 1 black pod

2 whole star anise

1½ teaspoons Shaoxing cooking wine or dry sherry

1 tablespoon dark soy sauce

2 teaspoons sea salt

3 to 7 spicy green chiles, sliced diagonally (in horse ears; see page 30)

In a pot of boiling water, parboil the chicken for 5 minutes. Drain in a colander and rinse off residue.

In a wok over high heat, heat the peanut oil until shimmering. Add the ginger and chicken, and stir-fry until the chicken is browned, about 5 minutes.

Add the cassia bark, cardamom, and star anise. Stir-fry for 1 to 2 minutes.

Add the cooking wine, soy sauce, and salt, and stir-fry for 1 minute.

Add 2 cups of water and slowly bring to a simmer. Add as many or as few chiles as you want for spiciness. Simmer for 20 to 25 minutes. Serve hot.

STEAMED CHICKEN
WITH PICKLED CHILES

Suān Là Zhēng Jī 酸辣蒸鸡

FAMILY: ZHOU JUXIANG 周菊香 | CHANGSHA, HUNAN

This dish was one of my favorite discoveries while traveling in Hunan. Before then, I'd never tried a flavor or dish like this one, and in that region I watched it being prepared in several households. To eat it was to ask yourself, "Now why didn't I think of that?" It's an impressive but simple dish filled with flavor that will surely transport your taste buds far from home.

Special equipment: bamboo steamer basket or pressure cooker

1 tablespoon fermented black beans (page 20)

1½ pounds chicken, skin on, cut into 1-inch pieces

2 teaspoons sea salt

½ teaspoon dark soy sauce

7 pickled chiles, sliced

Mince the beans.

In a medium mixing bowl, toss the chicken with the beans, salt, and soy sauce. Put the chicken in a medium heatproof bowl and top with the pickled chiles.

Set up the bamboo steamer basket in a wok. (If using a pressure cooker, insert a wire rack or shelf.) Heat the wok over high heat, fill with about 2 inches of water, and bring the water to a boil. Place the chicken in its heatproof bowl in the steamer basket. Turn the heat to low, cover the wok, and steam for 30 minutes (or for 12 minutes in the pressure cooker). Uncover the wok and carefully lift the bowl of chicken out of the steamer. Serve with a gentle warning to guests that the bowl is hot!

SERVING TIP: Top with a few soaked fermented black beans and a few slivers of scallion for color.

LESSONS IN CHENGDU

In 2007, a visit to Chengdu with my nephew barely hinted at the flavors and characters I would come to discover in the years ahead. The difference between traveling guided by a Lonely Planet book versus traveling guided by locals can best be described as, "Was blind, but now I see." Restaurateur and blogger Jiang Yi (see page 108) introduced me to Wang Ayi and her daughter, Yang Hongying, in Chengdu. As Wang Ayi prepared and cooked simple, famous Sichuan dishes, Hongying introduced each dish speaking a mixture of Chinese and English.

The kitchen was spacious, clean, and bright, and the counter was lined with bowls of ingredients. Wang Ayi used her left hand to mince pork for Old Wife Ma Po's Tofu (page 110). She expertly used her cleaver to scoop the meat into a bowl, keeping some on the blade to spread a little umami onto the fish waiting to steam for another dish. Hongying asked me if American people steam food, and I rattled off a list of foods often steamed—broccoli, crab, clams. These family visits gave my hosts and me fascinating opportunities to demystify our respective cultures.

Fish Soup with Pickled Mustard Greens (page 124) is a popular dish in Sichuan, and another recipe I learned with these new friends. Wang Ayi pickles her own mustard greens and peppers, and makes a chili bean paste that she stores in earthenware pickling jars on the balcony.

One story behind this dish tells of a servant who pickled vegetables with salt after noticing fellow servants struggling to eat old vegetables. He soaked them in salt and water for several days, and discovered that old vegetables were delicious when preserved like that. So they used them in many recipes thereafter. Another story says that a fish was once dropped accidentally into a soup of pickled mustard greens, thereby giving rise to this dish.

Hongying shared endearing details about herself and her family as the cooking lessons progressed—like that fact that she enjoys

Jiang Yi; Wang Ayi; the author; Hongying; and the author's assistant Juling He. Jiang Yi, a food blogger and restaurateur, introduced me to Chengdu host Wang Ayi and her daughter Hongying.

listening to Lady Gaga. During holidays, when the family members come together, all the men cook together. Jiang Yi, the only male in the room when I was there, didn't take the backstage while Wang Ayi cooked. He sliced the fish for the soup, chopped the chicken into 1-inch pieces for the Crispy Chicken with Red Chiles (page 86), and tossed the pieces into the bubbling oil that crisped the outside while creating a moist and tender center.

The red chile peppers blazed in the wok, and the stinging, spicy aroma emanated from the wok and filled the kitchen. The rest of us stepped away from the stove, but the cook stayed, squinting his eyes while tossing the chicken pieces hastily, lest the chiles blacken and burn.

Hongying watched as her mother patted together glutinous rice wormwood cakes and Wang Ayi explained that in recent years, the wormwood herb had become more scarce in Sichuan markets. At the end of the meal, we ate these herbaceous cakes as though devouring as many as possible would keep them from disappearing. I wanted to remember how these endangered specialties tasted, in perhaps the same way my dad remembers movie theaters charging a dime for two special features, a newsreel, and popcorn.

As ingredients like this vanish from market stalls, I fear that the repertoire of homestyle recipes is departing with them. Busy lives, urbanization, and the ease of consuming ready-made foods can make special treats such as these fade into a thing of the past.

> **"These family visits gave my hosts and me fascinating opportunities to demystify our respective cultures."**

Top to bottom: Wang Ayi's homemade pickled mustard greens. Wang Ayi slicing the pickled mustard greens for Fish Soup with Pickled Mustard Greens. Dried chile peppers being stir-fried for Crispy Chicken and Red Chiles.

CRISPY CHICKEN AND RED CHILES

Là Zi Jī 辣子鸡

FAMILY: WANG SHULING 王淑玲 | CHENGDU, SICHUAN

When eating this dish in Chinese restaurants, I have often found myself spending too much time hunting for chicken pieces among large lantern chiles and a sea of numbing Sichuan peppercorns. This dish is so much better when cooked at home, because you won't be cutting costs and skimping on the chicken. The dish zings from the peppercorns and the toasty heat of chiles are a nice accompaniment without overpowering the dish.

FOR THE CHICKEN

2 pounds chicken, cut into 1-inch pieces

3 tablespoons Shaoxing cooking wine or dry sherry

3 tablespoons dark soy sauce

1 cup potato starch

1 tablespoon freshly ground Sichuan peppercorns

1 tablespoon ground red chili powder or cayenne pepper

2 teaspoons sea salt

Peanut oil, for deep-frying

FOR THE SAUCE

10 cloves garlic, sliced

1 teaspoon freshly ground Sichuan peppercorns

3 tablespoons chili bean paste

2 tablespoons minced peeled fresh ginger

¼ teaspoon sea salt

1 cup dried red chiles

TO MAKE THE CHICKEN

In a large bowl, add the chicken pieces, cooking wine, and soy sauce, toss to coat, and let sit to marinate while you prepare the rest of the dish.

In a small, shallow bowl, combine the potato starch, ground peppercorns, chili powder, and salt.

Remove the chicken from the marinade, a few pieces at a time (shaking off excess marinade), dredge in the spiced starch mixture, and put on a plate.

In a wok over high heat, add 2 inches of peanut oil and heat until the oil shimmers. Fry the chicken, turning occasionally, for about 10 minutes until golden. (If you have an instant deep-fry thermometer, a reading for chicken doneness should be between 350 and 375°F.) Deep-fry the chicken in two to three batches, allowing enough room for the chicken to cook on all sides. As they cook, drain the chicken pieces on a paper towel–lined plate. Once all the chicken is fried, transfer the remaining oil to a heat-proof jar or bowl. Return 3 tablespoons of oil to the wok.

With the wok still on high heat, heat the peanut oil until shimmering. Add the garlic and stir-fry until fragrant, about 10 seconds. Add the ground peppercorns, chili bean paste, and ginger, and stir-fry until the sauce becomes a saffron red.

Return the chicken pieces to the wok and toss to coat with the sauce. Add the salt and dried red chiles, and stir-fry for 2 minutes. Serve hot.

COOKING TIP: If you give the chicken plenty of space in the frying process, the center will stay tender while the outside becomes crisp.

SUBSTITUTION TIP: You can replace the potato starch with cornstarch.

SERVING TIP: If you can find large, dried Sichuan chile peppers (also known as lantern chiles), scatter a couple handfuls into a deep serving dish. Then serve this dish over the chiles. This way, you will experience what I did in China—hunting for chicken in a sea of dried chiles—but with more chicken!

PAPAYA BRAISED CHICKEN

Mù Guā Dùn Jī 木瓜炖鸡

FAMILY: ZHANG BOWEI 张伯伟 | GAOMING, GUANGDONG

Papaya is known in Chinese culture as wonderfully beneficial for the skin. This stew is filled with medicinal goodness: papaya for healthy skin, codonopsis root for for managing and reducing stress, and goji berries (also known as wolfberries) known for their anti-aging properties and ability to balance *qi*, or life force. I learned to make this light chicken soup in Guangdong province. The papaya will have a slight sweetness, but in a soup it will seem more like a squash. Because of its cooling properties in Chinese herbal medicine, it is typically enjoyed during warm weather. The dipping sauce is for the chicken.

FOR THE SOUP

2 pieces dried codonopsis root or ginseng

2 tablespoons dried goji berries

2 pounds chicken, skinned if desired, boned, and cut into 2-inch pieces

1 large ripe papaya, cut into 2-inch cubes

2 (1-inch) pieces peeled fresh ginger, thinly sliced

1 teaspoon sea salt

¼ teaspoon freshly ground white pepper

FOR THE DIPPING SAUCE (OPTIONAL)

1 tablespoon cilantro, leaves and stems, roughly chopped

2 scallions, chopped

2 tablespoons peanut oil

2 tablespoons soy sauce

TO MAKE THE SOUP

In a soup pot over high heat, add 6 cups of water, codonopsis root, and goji berries. Bring the pot to a boil, then reduce the heat to medium-low and simmer for 10 minutes. Boiling the goji berries and codonopsis root before adding the other ingredients in this dish gives them time to release their medicinal properties.

In another large pot, add water almost to the top and bring to a boil over high heat. Add the chicken and parboil for 5 minutes. Drain and rinse the chicken.

Add the chicken to the first soup pot with codonopsis root, goji berries, and ginger. Bring to a boil, reduce the heat to medium-low, and simmer for 20 minutes. Add the papaya, and simmer for 10 minutes. Add the salt and pepper, and stir.

Serve warm.

Place the cilantro and scallions in a small heatproof bowl.

In a wok over high heat, heat the peanut oil until it starts to shimmer. Carefully pour the hot oil over the cilantro and scallions. Add the soy sauce and stir to combine.

SUBSTITUTION TIP: Despite its slightly bitter flavor, ginseng is buzzing with benefits, from boosting energy to lowering cholesterol and reducing stress. You can find it in most health food stores, so between its accessibility and health perks, I'd do my best to not leave it out. But if you don't have codonopsis or ginseng, the dish won't suffer too much.

COOKING TIP: Take extra care not to overcook the ripe papaya because it can get mushy.

KUNG PAO CHICKEN

Gōng Bǎo Jī Dīng 宫保鸡丁

FAMILY: ZHANG LIN 张林 | SUIJIANG, YUNNAN

Ah, yes, this favorite has traveled many years and long distances, and arrived on our plates in myriad variations. Kung Pao Chicken—or *Gong Bao Ji Ding*—is named after a Gongbao (palace guard) from the Qing dynasty named Ding Baozhen, who invented the dish in Sichuan. Using the freshly ground Sichuan peppercorns, plus sliced scallions, peanuts, dried red Sichuan chile peppers, and chicken, Ding managed to impress his house guests despite his limited resources after being ousted as a Shandong province official. Kung Pao Chicken fits within *hu la wei xing*, a Chinese cooking style that is characterized by scorched chilies. If you like your chicken spicy, use 1 heaping tablespoon of chili bean paste (see page 18). Serve this dish with Steamed Rice (page 36).

FOR BOWL ONE

1 pound skinless chicken breast, diced into ½-inch cubes

1 tablespoon Shaoxing cooking wine or dry sherry

1 tablespoon potato starch

1 teaspoon sea salt

1 heaping tablespoon fermented chili bean paste (optional)

FOR BOWL TWO

1 tablespoon potato starch

3 cloves garlic, thinly sliced

1 teaspoon sugar

1 teaspoon sea salt

1 tablespoon soy sauce

1 tablespoon Chinkiang vinegar or balsamic vinegar

1 large scallion or leek, white and green parts, chopped (the quantity depends on your taste)

2 red bell peppers, diced

½ cup roasted skinless peanuts

FOR THE WOK

4 tablespoons peanut oil

2 dried red chile peppers

½ tablespoon whole Sichuan peppercorns

TO MAKE BOWL ONE

In a medium bowl, combine the chicken, cooking wine, potato starch, salt, and chili bean paste (if using). Toss to thoroughly coat the chicken pieces. Set aside.

TO MAKE BOWL TWO

In a large bowl, add the potato starch and 2 tablespoons of cold water and stir to combine. Add the garlic, sugar, salt, soy sauce, and vinegar, and stir until blended. Add the scallion, sweet red peppers, and peanuts.

TO COOK IN THE WOK

In a wok over high heat, heat the peanut oil until it shimmers. Stir-fry the chile peppers and Sichuan peppercorns until fragrant, about 15 seconds.

Add the chicken mixture from bowl one and stir-fry for about 1 minute, keeping the chicken pieces separated so they brown evenly on all sides.

Add the mixture from bowl two and stir-fry for 1 more minute until cooked. Be sure not to overcook the chicken.

Transfer to a serving dish. Serve hot.

INGREDIENT TIP: Use freshly wok-fried peanuts if available. I like to buy peanuts already roasted, then toss them in the wok for 1 to 2 minutes to ensure a fresh roasted flavor. Also, sugar is essential for the balance of flavors. The recipe I learned uses 1 tablespoon of sugar. I reduced the amount from 1 tablespoon to 1 teaspoon here, but feel free to increase the amount if you prefer a sweeter Kung Pao Chicken.

ONE YOUNG COOK STANDS OUT

Beijing, like many major cities, is full of movers and shakers. It is also filled with many young people who work hard, party hard, and express themselves fashionably.

Jixing Zhang, who also went by her Western name Jessie, was one of those young women—she rocked brand names from head to toe, worked in hospitality, and learned some skills in marketing and tourism. She had once worked for the popular restaurant and cooking school Black Sesame Kitchen, founded by Jennifer Lin Liu (author of *Serve the People*). When Jessie had the opportunity, she started her own cooking school, Fang Jia Kitchen. She stood out to me because most young Chinese people around her age who I had met didn't know how to cook yet, and seemed to feel it just wasn't their time to learn.

> **"She stood out to me because most young Chinese people around her age who I had met didn't know how to cook yet."**

I rode my scooter to Jessie's peaceful *hutong* cooking school, a cozy dining room adjacent to a small kitchen. I was there on assignment, exploring cooking classes in Beijing for a story I was writing for *Time Out*.

Jessie started the class by introducing essential seasonings and ingredients. She then talked through the steps of making handmade noodles and Three-Colored Shredded Chicken (recipe on following page). The class was intimate, hands on, and easy to follow along.

These activities are one of the things I miss about Beijing. There were classes on many aspects of Chinese culture and all I had to do was hop on a bike or take a taxi to my next eye-opening adventure nestled in the alleyways of the capital.

Top to bottom: Jessie Zhang founder of Fang Jia Kitchen; Jessie starts her cooking lessons with a little background on Chinese food and culture.

THREE-COLOR SHREDDED CHICKEN

Sān Sè Jī Sī 三色鸡丝

FAMILY: JIXING ZHANG 张际星 | BEIJING

Simple enough to teach people new to Chinese cooking, this three-colored dish is a quick and easy stir-fry that uses a scallion-ginger-garlic flavor medley. Celtuce is a lettuce-like vegetable enjoyed for its long stem. It can be found in Asian supermarkets.

2 boneless chicken breasts

FOR THE MARINADE

1 egg white, beaten

1 tablespoon potato starch

1 teaspoon Shaoxing cooking wine or dry sherry

1 teaspoon sea salt

FOR THE STIR-FRY

1 cup celtuce or green bell pepper, julienned

1 cup carrot, julienned

2 tablespoons peanut oil

1 scallion, finely chopped

1 (1-inch) piece peeled fresh ginger, minced

2 cloves garlic, minced

1 tablespoon Shaoxing cooking wine or dry sherry

1 teaspoon sugar

1 teaspoon sea salt

½ teaspoon ground white pepper

Firm up the chicken in the freezer for 15 minutes to make it easier to slice. First cut the chicken into slices, then cut the slices into ¼-inch-thick strips.

TO MAKE THE MARINADE

In a medium bowl, combine the egg white, potato starch, 1 tablespoon of water, cooking wine, and salt. Add the chicken and toss to coat. Let the chicken marinate while you prepare the other ingredients.

TO MAKE THE STIR-FRY

Julienne the celtuce and carrot in strips the same size as the chicken.

In a wok over high heat, heat the peanut oil until it shimmers. Add the chicken pieces and stir-fry until they separate from each other, about 1 minute. Add the scallion, ginger, and garlic, and stir-fry for 1 minute. Add the celtuce and carrot. Add the cooking wine, sugar, salt, and pepper. Stir-fry for 2 minutes.

Transfer the chicken to a serving plate, and serve hot.

COOKING TIP: Sharpen your knife or cleaver in advance and it will be easier to cut chicken into thin strips, more so when the chicken is chilled until firm.

SUBSTITUTION TIP: Celtuce can also be replaced with julienned broccoli stems or celery. For the carrot, you can substitute red bell pepper. The key to this dish is the three colors: yellow, green, and orange (or red).

SAND GINGER STEAMED CHICKEN

Shā Jiāng Jú Jī 沙姜焗鸡

FAMILY: CHEN QIUFAN 陈秋凡 | FOSHAN, GUANGDONG

This dish offers a fragrance you can't get with other ingredients. To really ensure the best flavor, don't replace the sand ginger with galangal (Thai ginger) or everyday ginger. Turmeric won't work either. You can find fresh sand ginger in Southeast Asia, but in the United States, you will probably only find dried sand ginger in Asian grocery stores. To use dried sand ginger in this recipe, soak it in water overnight. Use good-quality 100 percent peanut oil, because it imparts a warm aroma and flavor that will make this dish a family favorite. And yes, the chicken really cooks in 20 minutes.

Special equipment:
Large rice cooker
(large enough to fit a
5-pound chicken)

1 (4- to 5-pound) whole chicken

2 (2-inch) pieces sand ginger, minced

4 tablespoons soy sauce

3 tablespoons peanut oil

1 teaspoon sea salt

Rinse the chicken inside and out and pat the outside dry. Don't dry the inside of the chicken, because the moisture will help facilitate steaming in the rice cooker.

In a small bowl, combine the sand ginger, soy sauce, peanut oil, and salt. Rub the chicken all over with the mixture, both inside and out.

Place the chicken in the rice cooker and turn it on. The chicken will be done when the rice cooker stops (15 to 20 minutes).

SERVING TIP: Serve this specialty with Steamed Rice (page 36), and leafy greens stir-fried with a little garlic. It's a lovely, simple meal.

SESAME CHICKEN

Zhī Ma Jī Kuài 芝麻鸡块

There's a good reason this dish is such a favorite. Sesame fried chicken offers a feast for the senses through its aroma, flavor, and texture that will please all at your dinner party. I like to serve this dish as the tried-and-true staple in a Chinese meal alongside other dishes that may require a more adventurous spirit. You can also serve this treat as an appetizer with toothpicks.

1 pound skinless chicken thigh meat, cut into 1-inch pieces

1 tablespoon Shaoxing cooking wine or dry sherry

1 tablespoon black or white sesame seeds

½ teaspoon sea salt

3 tablespoons potato starch

1 clove garlic, minced

¼ teaspoon ground white pepper

1 egg, beaten

2 cups peanut oil

In a medium mixing bowl, combine the chicken with the cooking wine, sesame seeds, and salt.

In a small bowl, mix together the potato starch, garlic, white pepper, and egg. Pour over the chicken and toss to coat. Let sit to marinate.

In a wok over high heat, add the peanut oil. When the oil shimmers, reduce the heat to medium and fry the chicken pieces until golden, about 5 minutes. Work in small batches to avoid crowding the pan so the chicken will be crisp.

Transfer the chicken to a paper towel–lined plate to drain.

Place the chicken on a serving plate and serve hot.

SERVING TIP: Serve the chicken atop a bed of julienned scallions, and accompany it with a dipping sauce that combines Scorched Chili Oil (page 37), soy sauce, and a dash of Chinkiang vinegar or balsamic vinegar.

MEAT

Old Wife Ma Po's Tofu (page 110)

DRY-FRIED BEEF

Gān Biān Niú Ròu 干煸牛肉

Beef isn't used widely in China because it's expensive to raise and to buy. But when Chinese cooking methods are applied to beef via a good stir-fry and key flavorings, the result is delicious. Try this quick stir-fry filled with umami and black bean flavor, and serve it with steamed rice for a satisfying meal.

8 ounces beef fillet

2 tablespoons Shaoxing cooking wine or dry sherry

1 tablespoon soy sauce

1 teaspoon potato starch

½ teaspoon sugar

2 teaspoons fermented black beans (page 20)

4 tablespoons peanut oil

1 teaspoon Sichuan peppercorns (page 23)

2 cloves garlic, minced

1 (1-inch) piece peeled fresh ginger, minced

5 dried red chiles (page 20), torn in half

1 tablespoon Scorched Chili Oil (page 37)

4 ounces fresh bean sprouts

1 tablespoon dark soy sauce

2 scallions, finely chopped

Cut the beef into strips 2 inches long and as thin as possible. Try to match the shape of the bean sprouts.

In a small bowl, combine the cooking wine, soy sauce, potato starch, and sugar, and stir to mix well. Set aside.

In another small bowl, soak the fermented black beans in warm water for 5 minutes, and then drain and chop finely. Set aside.

In a wok over medium heat, heat the peanut oil until it shimmers. Add the Sichuan peppercorns and stir-fry until fragrant, about 15 seconds. Using a slotted spoon, remove the peppercorns and discard. Turn up the heat to high (until it just starts to smoke), add the beef, and stir-fry for 2 minutes. Transfer the beef to a strainer to drain over a medium bowl, reserving the oil.

Return 2 tablespoons of drained peanut oil to the wok and heat. Add the garlic and ginger, and stir-fry until fragrant, about 10 seconds. Add the dried chiles, scorched chili oil, fermented black beans, bean sprouts, and dark soy sauce, and stir-fry for 1 minute.

Return the beef to the wok, and continue stir-frying for 1 minute. Add the wine sauce mixture, and continue stir-frying until most of the sauce has evaporated, about 1 minute.

Stir in the chopped scallions. Serve hot.

COOKING TIP: Put the beef in the freezer for 15 minutes to make it firm and easy to slice into thin strips.

STIR-FRIED BEEF WITH CELERY

Niú Ròu Sī Chǎo Qīng Cài 牛肉丝炒青菜

FAMILY: LIU MINGQIAN 刘明谦 | SUIJIANG, YUNNAN

This dish, with tender strips of beef, the heat of chili bean paste, and the zing of Sichuan peppercorns, tells a flavor story from the border between the Sichuan and Yunnan regions. Liu Shushu, who showed me this recipe, lived with his ethnically Sichuanese family in Suijiang, within Yunnan province. Sichuan food is fiery from Sichuan peppercorns, chili bean paste, and chiles. Yunnan food is less commanding, and uses fresh produce more than the fermented ingredients favored by Sichuan cuisine. This recipe calls for pepperoncini, the Italian pickled pepper mix available in the United States in jars. It is mildly spicy, and used for its sour-flavored heat. Liu Shushu used pickled green chiles that were from Yunnan yet tasted a lot like pepperoncini.

1 pound beef fillet

1 tablespoon chili bean paste

1 tablespoon soy sauce

2 teaspoons Shaoxing cooking wine or dry sherry

2 teaspoons potato starch

1 teaspoon sea salt, divided

2 stalks celery

6 pickled pepperoncini

2 tablespoons peanut oil

1 teaspoon Sichuan peppercorns

3 dried red chiles (page 20), snapped in two

⅔ cup chicken stock

Cut the beef into slices 2 inches long and ¼ inch thick. Place in a medium bowl and add the chili bean paste, soy sauce, cooking wine, potato starch, and ½ teaspoon of salt. Toss to combine well and allow the meat to marinate for 20 minutes.

Remove the celery threads and cut the stalks into diagonal slices ¼ inch thick. Thinly slice the pepperoncini diagonally.

In a wok over high heat, heat the peanut oil until it shimmers. Gently drop in the beef and stir-fry for 4 minutes. Transfer the beef to a strainer over a medium bowl, reserving the oil.

Return the oil to the wok. When it is hot, add the peppercorns and dried chiles and stir-fry for 10 seconds. Add the celery and pepperoncini, and stir-fry for 4 minutes.

Add the stock and bring the mixture to a simmer. Return the cooked beef to the wok, and stir-fry for 1 minute. Serve hot.

SUBSTITUTION TIP: The chiles are meant to add heat. If you don't like spicy, feel free to substitute a red bell pepper, which is sweet and will impart a mellower flavor and add color.

SPICY POACHED BEEF SLICES

Shuǐ Zhǔ Niú Ròu Piàn 水煮牛肉片

FAMILY: JIANG YI 蔣毅 | CHENGDU, SICHUAN

During the Song dynasty (960 to 1279) in the salt-producing city of Zigong, Sichuan, laborers used buffalo to power a well that extracted brine. When a buffalo was retired, it would be slaughtered to eat. Salt was abundant in the area, so the laborers boiled the beef in salt water with Sichuan peppercorns and chile peppers. The dish became a popular Sichuan dish. Because the beef was not stir-fried but boiled in a spicy broth, it became known as "water-boiled beef."

FOR THE BEEF AND MARINADE

½ pound beef fillet, thinly sliced

2 teaspoons potato starch

1 teaspoon Shaoxing cooking wine or dry sherry

½ teaspoon sea salt

FOR THE STIR-FRY

1 tablespoon peanut oil

4 celtuce or broccoli stem tips, sliced diagonally

3 stalks celery, threads removed and cut diagonally into thin slices

1 teaspoon sea salt

2 scallions, finely chopped

2 red chile peppers, such as serrano chiles, finely chopped

1 teaspoon green Sichuan peppercorns

5 tablespoons peanut oil, divided

4 cloves garlic, minced

2 (1-inch) pieces of ginger, minced

2 dried red chiles, torn in half

1 tablespoon chili bean paste

1 teaspoon green Sichuan peppercorns

1 tablespoon Shaoxing cooking wine or dry sherry

1 teaspoon dark soy sauce

1 large scallion, white parts, sliced, greens reserved for garnish

2 cups chicken stock

Sea salt

Combine the beef, potato starch, cooking wine, and salt, and toss to mix well. Let the beef marinate while you prepare the rest of the dish.

In a wok over high heat, heat the peanut oil until it shimmers. Add the celtuce, celery, and salt, and stir-fry until tender, about 2 minutes. Transfer the greens to a chopping board to cool. Chop the greens, then put in a medium heatproof bowl. Add the scallions, chile peppers, and green peppercorns to the bowl with the greens. In the wok, heat 4 tablespoons of peanut oil until shimmering, then pour over the mixture in the heatproof bowl.

In the wok, heat the remaining 1 tablespoon of peanut oil over high heat. When hot, add the garlic, ginger, dried red chiles, chili bean paste, and green peppercorns, and stir-fry until fragrant, about 1 minute. Add the beef and stir-fry for 1 minute, then add the cooking wine, soy sauce, and scallion, and stir-fry for 1 minute. Add the stock and bring to a boil, reduce the heat to low, and simmer for 10 minutes.

Season with salt, and drizzle with the scallion oil mixture. Serve hot in soup bowls.

SERVING TIP: Serve with Steamed Rice (page 36).

COOKING TIP: It is easier to slice the beef if the meat is placed in the freezer for 15 or 20 minutes before cutting. The meat will then be firm enough to slice thinly. It also helps to sharpen your knife in advance.

MIDDLE EASTERN INFLUENCES

Uyghurs are an ethnic group from Northwestern China in Xinjiang province. They are predominantly Muslim and are one of the 55 ethnic minorities living in China. Uyghur people are generally Central Asian; non-Chinese Uyghurs live in Uzbekistan, Kyrgyzstan, Kazakhstan, and Turkey.

When I visited Kashgar in the Xinjiang province, home to many Uyghurs, parts of this old city were being razed. The reasoning given to the residents was that the structures weren't seismically safe, so new, stronger multi-unit buildings would have to replace them. The government also gave incentives to Chinese from other regions to start businesses and settle in Xinjiang. Tractors and big trucks carrying produce and livestock traveled up and down the wide, newly paved roads. Billboards boasting the bounty of produce in the region flanked the roads. And of course, there were cranes and dust. Kashgar was definitely part of the changing China.

In Shanghai and Beijing, there were quite a few Uyghur restaurants where diners would be guaranteed belly-dancing, Middle Eastern musical entertainment, and rustic roasts—an undeniable contrast to mainstream Chinese culture. Kashgar was a different China, and it most certainly piqued my curiosity. I still hope to some day travel farther into Central Asia and the Middle East to dive even deeper into the titillating flavors and lively spirit of the Uyghur diaspora.

Uyghur food has decidedly Middle and Near Eastern roots. I was living in Shanghai when I had my first Uyghur lamb kebab seasoned with chili pepper, cumin, garlic, and salt. The flavor of these kebabs is one of my fondest food memories.

Below, left to right: The sizzling and steaming night market in Urumqi. A minaret illuminated in the evening near Id Kah Mosque in Kashgar.

XINJIANG LAMB KEBABS

Yáng Ròu Chuàn 羊肉串

I'll never forget walking along Wulumuqi Road in Shanghai and smelling something undeniably delicious being grilled. Grilled *anything* smells good, but grilled lamb spiced with cumin, chili, and sesame seed is irresistibly alluring. As the Uyghur men would fan the coals, the smoke carried with it a scent that drew me to this street food treat again and again. This recipe steals the show at a barbecue, so be sure to make enough kebabs! For these kebabs, use bamboo or metal skewers.

1 tablespoon red pepper flakes

1 tablespoon ground cumin

1 tablespoon white or black sesame seeds

3 cloves garlic, minced

1 teaspoon sea salt

2 pounds lamb shoulder chops

1 tablespoon peanut oil

With a mortar and pestle, grind together the red pepper flakes, cumin, sesame seeds, garlic, and salt until it all looks cracked and mixed. Reserve 1 tablespoon of the mixture in a small bowl.

Cut the lamb into 1-inch pieces, removing the bones (and discarding) and leaving the fat on, if desired, for added flavor. Place the lamb into a medium bowl and add the spice mix and the oil. Massage the spices into the meat, mixing well. Cover and marinate in the refrigerator for 3 hours or even overnight.

Thread the meat onto metal or bamboo skewers, stretching the meat out on the stick rather than keeping it in neat cubes.

Turn on the grill to high, and cook the lamb for 2 to 3 minutes on each side. Don't allow the flame to burn the meat. Cook until the meat and fat are nicely browned.

Transfer the skewers to a serving plate, sprinkle with the reserved spice mix, and serve.

INGREDIENT TIP: The meat of lamb shoulder chops requires a shorter amount of time to cook than some other cuts.

COOKING TIP: If using bamboo skewers, soak them in water overnight to prevent burning. If you have a mortar and pestle, it's the best tool for grinding the spices so the flavors really meld.

STIR-FRIED SHREDDED POTATO AND PORK

Ròu Sī Tǔ Dòu Sī 肉丝土豆丝

FAMILY: ZHU DANDAN 朱丹丹 | BEIJING

This dish reflects Zhu Dandan's consideration of the varying palates in her family. She and her kids loved the spicy-sour, stir-fried potato, but her husband did not like vinegar. Inspired by a delicious version of this dish at a restaurant, she figured out how to alter the recipe successfully without vinegar, so her whole family could enjoy the dish. The dish is a favorite in Beijing restaurants.

FOR THE PORK

½ pound pork loin, cut into thin strips

1½ teaspoons potato starch

1 teaspoon dark soy sauce

1 teaspoon Shaoxing cooking wine or dry sherry

FOR THE STIR-FRY

¾ pound potatoes, julienned

4 tablespoons peanut oil, divided

1 teaspoon Sichuan peppercorns

2 cloves garlic, minced

2 tablespoons soy sauce

½ teaspoon sea salt

1 scallion, finely chopped

TO MAKE THE PORK

Put the meat in the freezer for 20 minutes for easier cutting. Slice the meat against the grain, then cut each slice into thin strips.

In a small bowl, combine the meat, potato starch, dark soy sauce, and cooking wine, and toss to combine. Set it aside to marinate.

TO MAKE THE STIR-FRY

Soak the julienned potatoes in water for 30 minutes to remove extra starch. Drain in a colander, and put into a medium bowl. Add 1 tablespoon of peanut oil, and toss to coat.

In a wok over high heat, heat 1 tablespoon of peanut oil until it shimmers. Add the pork, and stir-fry it until the pieces separate from one another, about 2 minutes. Transfer to a strainer, drain, and set aside.

In the wok, add the remaining 2 tablespoons of oil. When hot, add the Sichuan peppercorns and stir-fry until fragrant, about 15 seconds. Using a slotted spoon, remove the peppercorns and discard. Add the garlic and potato, and stir-fry for 2 to 3 minutes. Add the soy sauce and stir-fry for 1 minute. Return the pork to the wok. Season with salt and stir-fry for 1 minute.

Sprinkle with the scallion, and serve hot.

VARIATION TIP: If you like a sour flavor—think fish and chips with malt vinegar—add 1 tablespoon of Chinkiang vinegar or balsamic vinegar 1 minute after stir-frying in the soy sauce.

COOKING TIP: Add the liquids slowly when stir-frying (not all at once), or your food will get soggy and not sear properly.

BRAISED EGG INGOTS AND PORK

Yuán Bǎo Ròu 元宝肉

FAMILY: ZHU DANDAN 朱丹丹 | BEIJING

This dish is typically called red-cooked pork (*hong shao rou*), but this variation also contains hard-boiled eggs. "Red-cooked"—or *hong shao*—is a typical way for Chinese to braise meat to enhance its appetizing dark color and taste. *Yuan bao* originally referred to the shape of money in ancient China, symbolized in this recipe by the eggs. Southern Chinese usually prepare *yuan bao rou* on the Lunar New Year's Eve—also known as the eve of the Chinese New Year—wishing the best for the next year's fortunes.

1 pound pork belly, cut into ½-inch pieces

1 tablespoon peanut oil

1 tablespoon sugar

2 tablespoons Shaoxing cooking wine or dry sherry

2 (1-inch) pieces peeled fresh ginger, julienned

1 scallion, julienned

2 whole star anise

1 bay leaf

2 (1-inch) pieces cassia bark or cinnamon bark

8 hard-boiled eggs, peeled

2 teaspoons sea salt

Parboil the pork for 5 minutes. Drain, rinse, and set aside in a bowl.

In a wok over high heat, heat the peanut oil until it shimmers. Reduce the heat to low. Add the sugar and stir until dissolved. Add the pork and increase heat to medium. Stir-fry for 5 minutes, coating the pork with the caramelized sugar.

Add the cooking wine, ginger, scallion, star anise, bay leaf, and cassia bark, and stir-fry for 1 to 2 minutes.

Using a small knife, pierce each hard-boiled egg ½ inch deep. Add the eggs and salt to the pork mixture in the wok. Reduce the heat to low. Add 2½ cups of hot water and let simmer for 90 minutes.

Discard the bay leaf and serve immediately.

SERVING TIP: This delicious comfort food is enjoyable over Steamed Rice (page 36). And don't forget to eat your veggies! Try serving this one with Dry-Cooked Green Beans (page 157) or Stewed Kale (page 156).

SHREDDED PORK AND SWEET PEPPERS

Tían Jião Ròu Sī 甜椒肉丝

FAMILY: JIANG YI 蒋毅 | CHENGDU, SICHUAN

This dish is a leaner version of Twice-Cooked Pork (page 113) and a bit less spicy. Jiang Yi taught me how to make this simple dish, and it stands out because the other dishes he taught me were so complex—delicious, but each one had special techniques, like taming flailing eels or beheading crayfish. It was an adventure in itself! But who can fault a passionate restaurateur and food blogger for wanting to share his favorite recipes, no matter how elaborate? This dish, however, is a quick stir-fry for an easy dinner with Sichuan flavor.

8 ounces pork loin

1 teaspoon potato starch

½ teaspoon sea salt

1 tablespoon soy sauce

2 large red bell peppers

2 tablespoons peanut oil

1 tablespoon chili bean paste

1 teaspoon minced peeled fresh ginger

1 teaspoon minced garlic

Slice the pork against the grain into ⅛-inch-thick pieces, then slice those into ⅛-inch strips.

In a bowl, combine 2 tablespoons of water, potato starch, salt, and soy sauce. Add the meat and mix well.

Julienne the bell peppers.

In a wok over high heat, heat the peanut oil until shimmering. Add the meat and stir-fry until the pieces separate from each other. Push the meat to the side of the wok.

Add the chili bean paste, ginger, and garlic and stir-fry to combine. Add the bell peppers, and stir-fry all ingredients together for 2 minutes, or until the peppers are cooked to your preferred tenderness.

Season with salt and serve immediately.

COOKING TIP: When slicing pork thinly, it is easier to do so if the meat is placed in the freezer for 15 or 20 minutes before cutting. It also helps to sharpen your knife.

THE GOOD, THE CHALLENGING, AND THE VERY TASTY

I owe a lot of my culinary journey to the families I found through social media. One such family was the brother-sister pair Jiang Yi and Jiang Li.

After posting my wish to meet families in the Sichuan region to learn their homestyle recipes, the enthusiastic and talented Jiang Yi of Chengdu responded immediately. Passionate about cooking, Jiang Yi opened the booming restaurant Hao Xia Zhuan, which literally translates to "ambitious legendary crayfish."

Beyond his restaurant, Jiang Yi has written extensively about the notoriously profitable hogwash oil industry in China—an illegal, unsavory business that collects restaurant waste, renders oil from it, and sells it to restaurants as cooking oil at very cheap prices. It was a secret practice until Jiang Yi helped expose it. He also introduced me to Xiao Ayi and Wang Ayi (page 84), two other wonderful hosts in Sichuan who taught me their favorite family recipes.

Jiang Yi's specialty is crayfish, which he and Jiang Li showed me how to cook in their small kitchen. Jiang Li led me to a Styrofoam box filled with more than 50 of the live crustaceans. She plucked out 28 crayfish, scrubbing their abdomens and yes, snipping off their antennae and heads. Jiang Yi then boiled up a stock in which he'd already cooked over 100 pounds of crayfish. With each boil, he only added more crayfish, seasoning, and water. The accumulating flavor trumped any seafood boil I've ever tasted.

While crayfish are Jiang Yi's specialty, I will always remember him for teaching me how to cook Wriggling Eels. Much like in the beheading of the crayfish, the process of preparing these eels was not for the faint of heart. Bought fresh and live, Jiang Yi let the eels swim in a large bowl until a wok filled with water was boiled. He released the eels into the wok and kept them submerged with a colander to keep them from lashing, until the

Jiang Yi and his sister Jiang Li.

might of their struggle was felt no longer. Once boiled, he rinsed them and then stir-fried them with veggies until they coiled.

This dish was an entirely new experience. I have eaten all manner of food from the land and sea, prepared in myriad ways. But eating eel in this fashion may not find an encore with me. Jiang Yi walked me through this very involved process; I was instructed to hold the head in one hand, the body in the other, and bite deep into the neck—enough to break off the head. Using my thumbs, I found the point where the flesh separated naturally from the spine and innards. I pulled away the spine and innards, and then ate the meat, which was a lot like firm fish.

But there were many memorably appealing recipes to be had as well. Of all the dishes Jiang Yi shared with me from his culinary repertoire (or menagerie), my favorite is Braised Pork Ribs in Aromatic Sauce (page 111)—a savory stew of battered-then-fried pork ribs with a smell reminiscent of a night-bazaar spice stall. After eating six ribs, my fingers were marinated. The next morning, I rubbed my face and was once again under the redolent spell of the spiced ribs.

> "While crayfish are Jiang Yi's specialty, I will always remember him for teaching me how to cook Wriggling Eels."

Top to bottom: Live eels. Jiang Yi commands a blazing stir fry. Eels coil in the heat of a hot stir fry.

OLD WIFE MA PO'S TOFU

Má Pó Dòu Fu 麻婆豆腐

FAMILY: WANG SHULING 王淑玲 | CHENGDU, SICHUAN

I thought I knew what *Ma Po Do Fu* was, until I had the real thing in Chengdu. Going to the Asian food aisle in a Western supermarket and picking up a packet of Ma Po Tofu instant sauce for your hamburger meat won't do justice to the authentic Ma Po Dou Fu. Sichuan peppercorn is the magic spice I'd been missing until I moved to China. It numbs the pang of heat from the chiles, and suffuses the olfactories and taste buds with a woody-pine floral flavor. This nineteenth-century dish is a famous Chengdu dish once served by Lady Chen, whose face was scarred with pock marks. All the fame and deliciousness of her tofu couldn't bring her a better name, but one would be hard-pressed to find a household in Chengdu unable to whip up a plate of Ma Po Dou Fu. Serve this dish over Steamed Rice (page 36).

2 tablespoons peanut oil

8 ounces lean ground pork

3 tablespoons chili bean paste

2 tablespoons fermented black beans

1 teaspoon red pepper flakes

1 tablespoon dark soy sauce

1 cup chicken stock

1 (14-ounce) box firm tofu, cut into 1-inch cubes

1 teaspoon peeled fresh ginger, minced

1 teaspoon potato starch

1 teaspoon freshly ground Sichuan peppercorns

1 scallion, green part, chopped

In a wok over medium-high heat, heat the peanut oil until shimmering. Add the pork and stir-fry until it breaks up and separates. Stir in the chili bean paste, black beans, red pepper flakes, soy sauce, and stock. Add the tofu and ginger, and stir-fry gently to keep the tofu from breaking up, for 1 minute. Reduce the heat to low, and simmer for 5 minutes.

In a small bowl, combine 2 tablespoons of cold water and potato starch. Turn up the heat under the wok to medium-high, and add the water-starch mixture. Stir-fry for 1 minute, then remove from the heat.

Sprinkle with the ground Sichuan peppercorns and garnish with chopped scallion. Serve hot.

COOKING TIP: Sichuan peppercorns can be ground in a spice grinder or a clean coffee grinder. If you don't have Sichuan peppercorns, you can leave it out.

BRAISED PORK RIBS IN AROMATIC SAUCE

Jiàng Xiāng Pái Gǔ 酱香排骨

FAMILY: JIANG YI 蒋毅	CHENGDU, SICHUAN

According to Jiang Yi, the enthusiastic chef who taught me how to cook this aromatic delight, this recipe is originally from Shandong. Jiang Yi's friend once cooked it for him, and he's been cooking it ever since. After opening spice containers holding bay leaves, star anise, Sichuan peppercorns, black cardamom, *Angelica dahurica* root, and fennel seed, the scents may make you feel like you're in a Chinese herbal medicine shop. The medicinal powers in this recipe are in fact plentiful and the ingredients can help cure a cold or end a headache. It's also delicious. In fact, this dish seduces while it simmers, leaving you waiting anxiously for one tummy-grumbling hour. The meal is worth the wait.

Special equipment: clay pot or Dutch oven

FOR THE RIBS

2 pounds pork spareribs, cut into 2-inch pieces

1 egg, beaten

5 tablespoons potato starch

1 teaspoon sea salt

Peanut oil

FOR THE BRAISING

2 teaspoons sugar

1 large scallion, white part, sliced diagonally

1 (1-inch) piece peeled fresh ginger, sliced

1 teaspoon green Sichuan peppercorns

2 tablespoons dark soy sauce

2 tablespoons chicken stock

1 teaspoon sea salt

3 whole star anise

5 bay leaves

4 slices dried *Angelica dahurica* root

2 black cardamom

1 teaspoon fennel seed

CONTINUED

BRAISED PORK RIBS IN AROMATIC SAUCE
CONTINUED

TO PREPARE THE RIBS

In a large pot of boiling water, parboil the pork ribs for 5 minutes. Drain and rinse the pork of bone bits and residue in cold water.

In a large bowl, combine the egg, potato starch, and salt. Add the pork and toss to coat evenly.

In a wok over low heat, add enough oil to deep-fry, about 2 inches, and heat until shimmering. Deep-fry the ribs in small batches until golden, about 3 minutes. Transfer the ribs to a plate, and retain 1 tablespoon of oil.

If using a clay pot, add 2 cups of water and slowly warm it up over low heat. If using a Dutch oven, heat 2 cups of water over low heat.

TO BRAISE

In the wok over medium-high heat, add the sugar. Stir until the sugar begins to melt. Add the scallion, ginger, and Sichuan peppercorns, and stir-fry for 1 minute. Add the pork ribs and stir-fry until the ribs are mostly coated with the glaze, about 3 minutes Add the soy sauce, stock, and salt, and stir-fry for 2 minutes.

Transfer the pork stir-fry to the clay pot or Dutch oven over medium-high heat. Add more water to almost cover the ribs. Add the star anise, bay leaves, *Angelica dahurica* root, black cardamom, and fennel seed. Bring to a boil, reduce the heat to low, and simmer for 45 minutes.

Season with salt, and serve immediately.

SERVING TIP: This stew is perfect on a cold, gray day. It will warm you right up.

INGREDIENT TIP: This stew is filled with aromatic spices with beneficial properties known in Chinese herbal medicine. The key ingredient here is *Angelica dahurica* root which can be found in Asian grocery stores or Chinese herbal medicine stores. But if you don't have any on hand, it's okay to leave it out—the stew will still be aromatic. *Angelica dahurica* root is believed to help remove dampness from the body to help with the common cold and to alleviate pain such as headaches.

TWICE-COOKED PORK

Huí Guō Ròu 回锅肉

FAMILY: CHEN YOU GUI 陈友贵 | SUIJIANG, YUNNAN

Generally, the twice-cooked pork in these recipes is pork belly that's boiled, then stir-fried with a fragrant chorus of chile peppers and bean pastes. This recipe may differ from other twice-cooked pork recipes. This is the version I learned from Liu Ayi during my memorable visit to Suijiang (see page 114). The thin, curled, green chile pepper in her lesson was about 4 inches long with wrinkled skin, and spicy. The red peppers were sweet.

1 pound pork belly, with the skin layer intact

5 spicy green chile peppers, such as fresh jalapeños or serranos

2 red bell peppers

3 large scallions, chopped

2 tablespoons peanut oil

1 tablespoon chili bean paste

1 (1-inch) piece peeled fresh ginger, minced

1 teaspoon Shaoxing cooking wine or dry sherry

1 teaspoon soy sauce

1 teaspoon sugar

Sea salt

Bring a large pot of water to a boil over high heat. Add the pork belly and return to a boil, then reduce the heat to low and simmer for 20 minutes. Remove the pork from the water and allow to cool. Once cooled, put the pork in the freezer for 20 minutes. This will make the meat firm and easy to slice thinly without the skin and fat breaking from the meat. Cut the cold pork belly into slices as thin as bacon slices, about 2 inches long by 1 inch wide.

Cut the chile peppers, bell peppers, and scallions diagonally (in horse ear slices; see page 30).

In a wok over high heat, heat the peanut oil until shimmering. Add the pork belly slices and stir-fry until the edges are slightly crisped and some of the fat has melted, about 4 minutes. Move the pork to the side of the wok.

Add the chili bean paste and stir-fry until the oil is fiery and fragrant. Add the chile peppers and red peppers, scallions, and ginger, and stir-fry.

Add the cooking wine, soy sauce, sugar, and season with salt. Serve immediately.

INGREDIENT TIP: Pork belly is sold in many supermarkets, but isn't usually sold in slabs unless you request it from the butcher. Uncured bacon can also be used, but avoid smoked or cured.

FOOD FOR RAISING SPIRITS

Though the six-lane highway from Yibin to Suijiang signaled healthy funding for public works, a markedly different state of affairs was revealed once our driver turned off the road. Following the Jinsha River, a segment of the Yangtze River, we passed small villages that appeared abandoned—buildings paneled with chipped and missing ceramic tiles, roads cratered with potholes, and an occasional resident peering from behind a glassless windowsill.

What had happened here? Was this a piece of China the authorities forgot? Why were these villages empty? I had a lot of questions for the uncle who was driving. Then I noticed an abandoned factory across the river.

My visit to Suijiang took place in July 2009. The Xiangjiaba Dam was set to be completed three years later, and waters from the Jinsha River would flood the entire valley. In preparation, many villages emptied; their folk moved to other towns or higher ground.

After the uncle parked and I got out, I noticed a white pillar gleaming against the lush green cornfield. It marked the level to which the water would rise. Families received ¥5,000 CNY (at the time, roughly $660 USD) per person to relocate—a pittance compared to the amount a family would need to invest in starting a new life.

From the hill where the Chen family lived, they could peer down into the valley awaiting to be submerged, then look upward to the cranes building a new town called Suijiang Hubinshengtai Xian.

The family's nephew, Chen Tianchong, viewed the rising waters with hope, as his line of work was remodeling homes. He welcomed the prospect of new business opportunities. He was 38 and lived on the second floor with his wife and daughter. At that time, business was very slow since no one had any interest in fixing anything before the flood. He looked forward to the ¥5,000 CNY stipend.

On the ground floor of the same building, Liu Ayi and Chen Shifu lived with their son, Chen

This page: Suijiang, the city that would be flooded, while the new Suijiang city was under construction at the top of the hill.

Opposite, clockwise: The Chen family with Chen Jian (son), Chen You Gui (father), and Liu Ming Fen (mother). After Liu Ayi taught the author four dishes, other family members brought more food for a large family-style lunch. Liu Ayi stir-frys using a portable burner.

Jian. Both Liu Ayi and her husband managed the cooking, but due to a recent traffic accident, Chen Shifu was now confined to a wheelchair and could only give directions. Liu Ayi appeared sullen throughout our visit. Their son was shy and smiled rarely, if at all. Ironically, it was Chen Shifu who seemed to bear the lightness in the family of three, pivoting about in his chair and explaining the ingredient names for each of the four dishes during the lesson.

Suijiang is in Yunnan province, but sits on the border next to Sichuan. Liu Ayi's family originates from Pingshan Xian in Sichuan. So although the family lives in Yunnan, culturally they are Sichuanese.

First to hiss on their wok was one of China's famous pork dishes, Twice-Cooked Pork (page 113). Liu Ayi tossed in a plate of red and green spicy chiles, and despite being in a large room with the front garage-sized door open, we still coughed from the chile-fumed air.

Liu Ayi added stir-fries of liver and leaves bleeding violet juice, green peppers with shredded pork, and pumpkin leaf shoots.

Recurring flavors of Sichuan peppercorns and dried chiles defined my first impressions of Liu Ayi's family recipes. As other family members joined us for lunch, more dishes were added to the spread. Greeting smiles arrived and as people filled the room, looming past and future tragedies were temporarily forgotten, reminding me once again of food's mighty ability to bring people together and raise collective spirits.

STIR-FRIED PORK WITH PICKLED MUSTARD GREENS

Méi Cài Chǎo Ròu 梅菜炒肉

FAMILY: ZHU LEQUAN 朱乐全 | KUNSHAN, JIANGSU

Pickled dried mustard greens (see page 21) are a common ingredient in Hakka cuisine. This stir-fry is a leaner and quicker variation of the well-known steamed pork belly dish. These greens are used especially for braising. Their flavor converges with the pork and soy sauce, resulting in a rich, aromatic dish.

4 ounces pickled dried mustard greens

8 ounces lean pork tenderloin

2 tablespoons peanut oil

1 (1-inch) piece peeled fresh ginger, slivered

1 tablespoon Shaoxing cooking wine or dry sherry

1 tablespoon dark soy sauce

2 teaspoons sugar

½ teaspoon sea salt

Soak the pickled dried mustard greens for 5 to 6 hours or overnight. Rinse the soaked greens in a large bowl of water five or six times, or in running water until it runs clear of sand and dirt. Drain and set aside. Julienne the mustard greens. Cut the pork into ⅛-inch-thick slices, then cut the slices into ⅛-inch strips.

In a wok over medium-high heat, heat the peanut oil until shimmering. Add the ginger and stir-fry until fragrant, about 15 seconds. Add the pork and stir-fry for 2 minutes. Add the cooking wine, and stir in the pickled greens and soy sauce. Continue to stir-fry for 2 minutes. Add 2 cups of water, reduce the heat to low, and simmer for 10 minutes.

Add the sugar and salt, and stir-fry until most of the water is absorbed by the meat and greens. Serve hot.

SERVING TIP: This dish is heavenly with a bowl of Steamed Rice (page 36).

RED-COOKED PORK SHANGHAI STYLE

Hóng Shāo Ròu 红烧肉

FAMILY: GONG DONGHUA 龚冬华 | SHANGHAI

I had never known a simple red-cooked pork belly recipe until the day I visited Chen Chen's family in Shanghai. The result of cooking pork belly in soy sauce, sugar, ginger, and star anise is pure deliciousness. Adding the cooking wine dispels any gamey flavor, according to Chen Chen's mother. Because this recipe is from Shanghai, the flavor reflects the region's preference for sweetness, shying away from garlic and strong-flavored spices. If your taste buds align with those in Shanghai, this recipe will surely please.

Special equipment: clay pot or Dutch oven

FOR PARBOILING THE PORK

3 pounds pork belly, with skin

6 (1-inch) pieces peeled fresh ginger, smacked

1 tablespoon Shaoxing cooking wine or dry sherry

FOR BRAISING THE PORK

4 tablespoons peanut oil

2 tablespoons Shaoxing cooking wine or dry sherry

2 tablespoons dark soy sauce

2 tablespoons chicken stock

2 tablespoons soy sauce

1 tablespoon sugar

¼ teaspoon sea salt

TO PARBOIL THE PORK

Bring a large pot of water to a boil over high heat. Immerse the slab of pork belly, and add the ginger and the cooking wine. Boil for 5 minutes, then drain and rinse the pork with cold water. Cut the pork belly into 1-inch cubes.

TO BRAISE THE PORK

In a wok over high heat, add the oil and heat until simmering.

Add the pork pieces and stir-fry until the cubes have seared on all sides, 4 to 5 minutes. Add the cooking wine and dark soy sauce, continuing to stir fry. Add 2 cups of water, stock, soy sauce, sugar, and salt, and bring to a boil. Reduce the heat to low, cover, and simmer for 2 to 3 hours.

Serve with the gravy from braising.

INGREDIENT TIP: The more clear the strata of five layers can be seen in the piece of pork belly, the better for this traditional dish. So when selecting a slab of pork belly, try to find one where the strata are even and evident.

SERVING TIP: Serve with rice, over noodles, or on top of a noodle soup. And by all means, keep all that gravy—it's gold! That's the addictive substance that smothers the rice with delicious glory.

PORK-STUFFED WHEAT GLUTEN BALLS

Ròu Niàng Miàn Jīn 肉酿面筋

FAMILY: XU WEIWEN 许伟文 | WUXI, JIANGSU

Fried gluten balls became popular during the Qianlong dynasty (mid- to late eighteenth century). They are characterized by their golden color, smooth exterior, and crispy texture. They are also rich in protein. I learned this recipe in Wuxi, a cultural, historical, and tourist hub on the Yangtze River where fried gluten balls are a local specialty. This dish is often served at holiday celebrations.

FOR THE STUFFED GLUTEN BALLS

1 pound ground fatty pork

2 (1-inch) pieces peeled fresh ginger, minced

1 scallion, minced

1 teaspoon sesame oil

1 teaspoon potato starch

1 heaping teaspoon sea salt

2 tablespoons Shaoxing cooking wine or dry sherry

10 fried gluten balls (see Ingredient Tip)

FOR THE BROTH

8 cups chicken stock

3 tablespoons dark soy sauce

2 tablespoons Shaoxing cooking wine

½ teaspoon sea salt

1 scallion, finely chopped, for garnish

Sesame oil, for garnish

TO MAKE THE GLUTEN BALL FILLING

In a mixing bowl, combine the pork, ginger, scallion, sesame oil, potato starch, salt, and cooking wine, and mix well to form a smooth, pasty texture. A stand-up mixer or food processor can achieve this more easily than vigorous hand mixing. Chill the mixture in the refrigerator for at least 1 hour.

TO MAKE THE GLUTEN BALLS

Holding one fried gluten ball in your hand, carefully use the index finger or thumb of the other hand to make a hole. Using chopsticks or something slender, gently stuff some filling into the gluten ball, being careful not to break the ball. There's no need to seal the ball closed. Stuff the remaining gluten balls.

TO MAKE THE BROTH

In a large soup pot over high heat, add the stock and bring to a simmer. Reduce the heat to low, then add the soy sauce, cooking wine, salt, and stuffed gluten balls. Cover and simmer for 25 minutes. Season with salt to taste.

Serve, garnished with the scallion and a drizzle of sesame oil.

INGREDIENT TIP: Fried gluten balls are sold in packages in Asian markets and on Amazon.

INGREDIENT TIP: When you shop for fatty ground pork, look for pork with more white specks of fat in the meat. You can also ask your butcher to grind a fattier cut.

SERVING TIP: Broth invites you to use your creative culinary imagination, so after 20 minutes of simmering the gluten balls, you might want to add some noodles, bok choy, bean sprouts, or anything else you like in a noodle soup. Then simmer for 5 to 10 minutes until the vegetables are cooked to your preference.

CHAPTER SEVEN

FISH & SEAFOOD

Red-Cooked Fish (page 122)

RED-COOKED FISH

Hóng Shāo Jì Yú 红烧鲫鱼

FAMILY: ZHOU JUXIANG 周菊香 | CHANGSHA, HUNAN

Red cooking is a delicious way to enjoy meat, but applying the flavors to fish permits you to experience this aromatic flavor much sooner, because fish cooks so quickly.

FOR THE FISH

1 tablespoon sea salt

1 teaspoon Shaoxing cooking wine or dry sherry

1 (1-pound) fish (bass or trout), cleaned and scaled

1 teaspoon fermented black beans

3 tablespoons peanut oil

3 (1-inch) pieces peeled fresh ginger, sliced

1 garlic chive, white part sliced (see Substitution Tip)

5 to 8 dried red chiles

1 tablespoon Shaoxing cooking wine or dry sherry

1 tablespoon dark soy sauce

1 teaspoon Chinkiang vinegar or balsamic vinegar

Sea salt

FOR THE GARNISH

1 tablespoon peanut or vegetable oil

1 red bell pepper, julienned

1 (1-inch) piece peeled fresh ginger, slivered

2 cloves garlic, sliced

TO MAKE THE FISH

Rub the salt and cooking wine on both sides of the fish. Marinate for 5 minutes.

In a small bowl, soak the beans in warm water for 5 minutes and drain.

In a wok over medium-high heat, heat the peanut oil until it shimmers. Shake any excess salt off the fish, and fry the fish until golden, about 3 minutes on each side. Add the ginger, garlic chive, chiles, and black beans, and stir to combine. Add 2 cups of water and bring to a quick boil, then reduce the heat to low and simmer. Add the cooking wine, dark soy sauce, and vinegar, and simmer for 5 minutes. Season with salt. Transfer the fish to an oval serving plate, and pour the broth over the fish. Rinse the wok and return it to the heat.

TO MAKE THE GARNISH

In the wok over high heat, heat the oil until shimmering. Add the bell pepper, ginger, and garlic, and stir-fry until fragrant, about 20 seconds. Remove from the heat and pour over the fish.

SUBSTITUTION TIP: You can often find garlic chives at your local farmers' market. If they are not available, you can substitute with scallions and a clove of garlic.

STEAMED FISH IN EGG CUSTARD

Jī Dàn Ān Gōng Yú 鸡蛋安公鱼

FAMILY: ZHANG ZHIYING 张志英 | WUXI, JIANGSU

This dish was originally prepared using a whole fish. It's delicious, but I find it easier to serve and eat when the fish is already boned and cut into pieces that are easy to pick up with chopsticks or serve with a spoon.

Special equipment: bamboo steamer or pressure cooker

3 eggs, beaten

½ teaspoon sea salt

1 tablespoon Shaoxing cooking wine or dry sherry

3 scallions, sliced diagonally

1 teaspoon peeled fresh ginger, slivered

¼ pound fish fillets (sea bass or trout), cut into 1-inch pieces

¼ teaspoon dark soy sauce

¼ teaspoon sesame oil

In a large bowl, combine the eggs, 1½ cups of water, salt, cooking wine, scallions, and ginger. Add the fish, and turn to coat on all sides. Pour into two bowls that will fit into your bamboo steamer.

In the wok over medium-high heat, fill with water to come up just below the steamer basket. Cover and steam for 15 minutes, or until the egg custard has set. You can test it by inserting a toothpick or the point of a knife, which should come out clean.

Remove the bowls from the steamer, drizzle with dark soy sauce and sesame oil, and serve hot.

SERVING TIP: Top with freshly chopped scallion and cilantro.

FISH SOUP WITH PICKLED MUSTARD GREENS

Suān Cài Yú 酸菜鱼

FAMILY: WANG SHULING 王淑玲 | CHENGDU, SICHUAN

This dish is typically Sichuan—a simple yet vibrant fish soup that awakens the palate with the flavors of pickled dried mustard greens (see page 21) and chiles. The defining ingredient here is the mustard greens. Without them, this famous Sichuan soup wouldn't be the same.

2 ounces pickled mustard greens

1 whole carp, bass, or trout (1½ pounds), cleaned, filleted, and cut into ½-inch slices (see Cooking Tip page 126)

1 egg white, beaten

4 tablespoons peanut oil

3 tablespoons minced fresh garlic

3 tablespoons peeled, minced fresh ginger

5 to 8 pickled chile peppers (see page 20)

2 teaspoons freshly ground white pepper

8 cups chicken stock

2 dried red chiles, broken in half

1 teaspoon Sichuan peppercorns (optional)

1 scallion, green part, chopped

Soak the pickled mustard greens in cold water for at least 10 minutes, then slice them into thin strips. Set aside.

Put the fish pieces in a bowl, add the egg white, and gently toss to coat the fish.

In a wok over medium-high heat, heat 2 tablespoons of peanut oil until shimmering. Add the garlic and ginger and stir-fry until fragrant, about 20 seconds. Add the pickled chile peppers, pickled mustard greens, and white pepper, and stir-fry for 1 minute.

Add the stock to the wok and bring to a boil, then reduce heat to low and simmer for 20 minutes. Lift the vegetables out of the broth to a serving bowl.

Add the fish pieces to the broth in the wok and boil for 2 minutes. Transfer the fish and broth to the serving bowl with the vegetables. Rinse and dry the wok. Return the wok to the heat.

Add the remaining 2 tablespoons of peanut oil, the red chiles, and the Sichuan peppercorns (if using), and heat until the mixture starts to sizzle, about 1 minute. Drizzle this mixture over the bowl of fish. Garnish with the chopped scallion and serve.

SUBSTITUTION TIP: If you can't find pickled chile peppers, use pickled Thai peppers. Both red chiles are thin and 1½ inches long when whole.

SPICY POACHED FISH

Shuǐ Zhǔ Yú 水煮鱼

FAMILY: ZHANG XINYU 张欣雨 | CHENGDU, SICHUAN

Water-Poached Fish is a common dish in Sichuan that found its place in the region during the 1980s, and later became a mainstay in China's restaurants and family tables. This dish treats guests to supple bites of tender fish served in a spicy-numbing broth, one of Sichuan's distinct flavors.

FOR THE FISH AND VEGETABLES

1 (2-pound) fish (striped bass or trout), cleaned and scaled, with fish head (See Cooking Tip)

1 tablespoon potato starch

1 tablespoon lemon juice

1 tablespoon peanut oil

3 slices peeled fresh ginger

2 stalks celery, diagonally sliced

¼ teaspoon sea salt

1 small cucumber, diagonally sliced

FOR THE BROTH

2 tablespoons peanut oil

1 tablespoon ginger, minced

1 tablespoon garlic, minced

3 scallions, white part, chopped (green part reserved for garnish)

2 tablespoons chili bean paste

6 cups chicken stock

2 teaspoons sea salt

FOR THE GARNISH

2 tablespoons peanut oil

1 tablespoon Sichuan peppercorns

1 tablespoon red pepper flakes

3 scallions, green part, chopped

CONTINUED

TO PREPARE THE FISH AND VEGETABLES

In a large shallow bowl, mix the potato starch and lemon juice, and add the fish. Marinate for 20 minutes.

In a wok, heat the peanut oil over medium-high heat until shimmering. Add the ginger and stir-fry until fragrant, about 10 seconds. Add the celery and stir-fry for 3 minutes. Add the salt. Transfer to a serving bowl and top with the fresh cucumber slices.

TO MAKE THE BROTH

In the wok, heat the peanut oil over medium-high heat until shimmering. Add the ginger, garlic, and scallion, and stir-fry for 30 seconds. Add the chili bean paste and stir-fry until the oil is fiery red and fragrant. Increase the heat to high, add the stock, fish head, and salt, and bring to a boil. Add the fish slices and boil gently for 10 minutes. Transfer the fish with the head to the large soup serving bowl, and pour in the broth.

TO MAKE THE GARNISH

In the wok, heat the peanut oil over medium-high heat until shimmering. When hot, remove from the heat and add the Sichuan peppercorns and red pepper flakes. After the oil mixture sizzles for 30 seconds, drizzle it over the bowl of fish.

Garnish with the chopped scallion greens, and serve hot.

SERVING TIP: Guests can serve themselves from a family-style bowl, or you can serve this dish in individual bowls.

COOKING TIP: To clean the fish, first remove the head, cutting just where the gills end. Set the head aside. Using a very sharp knife, cut from head to tail along the belly of the fish. Separate the flesh from the ribs on the underside and cut along the backbone on the upper side. Remove the backbone. Take half of the fish and lay it skin-side down. Pull out any bones you see. Angle your knife nearly flat as you cut the fish into thin slices. Repeat with the other half of the fish. Discard the skin. If your fishmonger can clean and debone the fish, that's helpful, but remind him to give you the head.

BRAISED FISH WITH SCALLIONS

Cōng Kǎo Jì Yú 葱烤鲫鱼

FAMILY: QUAN HUIYING 全慧英 | SHANGHAI

This recipe is simple, yet it is also a special dish to serve guests. Plus, it has super-stition embedded in its tradition: When one side of the fish is eaten, just remember not to flip the fish, since that symbolizes capsizing a boat, thus turning your luck. The proper way to continue eating the fish is simply to remove the whole backbone to get to the other side.

5 tablespoons peanut oil, divided

20 scallions, cut into 3-inch pieces

4 thumbnail-size slices peeled fresh ginger

1 (1-pound) fish (bass or trout), scaled and cleaned

2 tablespoons Shaoxing cooking wine or dry sherry

1 tablespoon dark soy sauce

½ teaspoon sea salt

1 teaspoon sugar

Heat 1 tablespoon of peanut oil in a wok over high heat. Add the scallions and stir-fry for 2 minutes. Transfer to a plate and set aside.

Reduce the heat under the wok. Add the remaining 4 table-spoons of oil and heat until shimmering. Add the ginger. Carefully place the whole fish into the wok and fry both sides until golden, about 3 minutes on each side. Add the cooking wine, soy sauce, salt, sugar, and 1 cup of water. Bring to a boil, then reduce the heat to low and simmer for 5 minutes. Turn the fish over. Return the scallions to the wok and simmer for 1 minute.

Carefully transfer the fish to a serving dish and top with the scallions and sauce. Serve hot.

VARIATION TIP: If you prefer, use fish fillets instead of a whole fish.

RED-COOKED EEL

Hóng Shāo Huá Shàn 红烧滑鳝

FAMILY: GONG DONGHUA 龚冬华 | SHANGHAI

Red-cooking is a classic technique in Chinese cuisine, and it's very tasty. While a typical red-cooked pork dish makes you wait at least an hour for its goodness, this dish, like the Red-Cooked Fish (page 122), satisfies you sooner. This is a warming delicacy, great over Steamed Rice (page 36), and sweetly reminiscent of my visit with Chen Chen's warm, hospitable family in Shanghai.

2 medium-hot green chiles such as Anaheim, seeded and sliced

3 tablespoons peanut oil

4 (1-inch) pieces fresh ginger, peeled and julienned

1½ pounds eel, cleaned and cut into 2-inch pieces (see Ingredient Tip)

1 tablespoon Shaoxing cooking wine or dry sherry

1 tablespoon soy sauce

1 tablespoon dark soy sauce

½ teaspoon sea salt

2 teaspoons sugar

In a large saucepan of water over high heat, parboil the green peppers for 1 to 2 minutes. Drain and set aside.

In a wok over medium-high heat, add the peanut oil and heat until shimmering. Add the ginger and stir-fry until fragrant, about 10 seconds. Add the eel, cooking wine, soy sauce, dark soy sauce, and 1 cup of water and stir to combine. Cover the wok, reduce the heat to low, and simmer for 10 minutes. Add the salt, sugar, and green chiles, and cook for 1 more minute.

Transfer the dish, including liquid, to a deep serving plate. Serve hot.

INGREDIENT TIP: In China, when you buy meat and seafood, you can request a specific cut for whatever dish you have in mind from butchers and fishmongers. Don't hesitate to ask your fishmonger to clean and cut the eel to your preference. To clean the eel, slit it down the belly, and remove the spine and innards and discard. Cut the eel into 2-inch pieces.

SALTWATER SHRIMP

Yán Shuǐ Xiā 盐水虾

If you love seafood, you'll appreciate this simple dish that relies on the freshness of the shrimp. It's best to cook the shrimp the same day you buy them. While the recipe is called Saltwater Shrimp, Gong Ayi, like most Shanghainese people, prefers the flavorful freshwater variety harvested in the ancient river town in the area. Shrimp cooked with their shells and heads are more flavorful. My mother always said, "Americans don't know what they're missing by removing the head." It took some time and the right dishes before I realized that the rich flavor of shrimp is in the head. And to the Shanghainese, there's more flavor in the freshwater shrimp head.

¼ cup sea salt plus 2 teaspoons, divided

1 pound freshwater shrimp

2 scallions, cut into 2-inch pieces

2 (1-inch) pieces fresh ginger, peeled and sliced

2 tablespoons Shaoxing cooking wine or dry sherry

2 teaspoons sea salt

In a large mixing bowl, mix ¼ cup of salt and 2 cups of water for the brine. Rinse the shrimp and add to the brine. Let sit for 30 minutes. Drain and rinse the shrimp.

In a wok over high heat, add 2 cups of water, the scallions, ginger, cooking wine, and the remaining 2 teaspoons of salt, and bring to a boil. Add the shrimp and return to a boil. Cook for 2 minutes. Remove from the heat, drain, and serve.

INGREDIENT TIP: Select shrimp with transparent shells, because this signifies freshness.

STIR-FRIED SHRIMP

Yóu Bào Xiā 油爆虾

FAMILY: QUAN HUIYING 全慧英 | SHANGHAI

Grass shrimp are found in fresh water from the river towns in China to the Chesapeake Bay. Freshwater shrimp are preferred for their sweeter flavor over saltwater shrimp. They have a delicate body with a serrated horn, and it's pointy, so be careful to not prick yourself. If you can't find this kind of shrimp, any medium-size shrimp will work. You'll get the most flavor if you retain the heads and shells.

¼ cup sea salt

1 pound grass shrimp,

2 to 3 tablespoons peanut oil

2 slices peeled fresh ginger

2 tablespoons soy sauce

1 tablespoon sugar

1 tablespoon Shaoxing cooking wine

2 scallions, finely chopped, green and white parts divided

In a large mixing bowl, mix 2 cups of water and the salt to make a brine, stirring to dissolve the salt. Trim the legs and any sharp ends off the shrimp. Rinse the shrimp and add to the brine. Let sit for 30 minutes. Drain and rinse the shrimp.

In a wok over medium-high heat, add the peanut oil and heat until shimmering. Add the ginger and stir-fry until fragrant, about 10 seconds. Add the shrimp and stir-fry until golden, about 3 minutes. Remove the shrimp to a plate and set aside.

To the wok, add the soy sauce, sugar, and cooking wine, and when it starts to simmer, return the shrimp to the wok. Toss in the white parts of the scallions. Stir-fry for 30 seconds, then transfer to a serving plate.

Garnish with the green parts of the scallion, and serve hot.

VARIATION TIP: The original recipe used 3 tablespoons of sugar. Shanghai cuisine is characteristically sweet. I find that the dish is sweet enough with just 1 tablespoon of sugar.

SILVER FISH AND EGG OMELET

Jī Dàn Chǎo Yín Yú 鸡蛋炒银鱼

FAMILY: ZHANG ZHIYING 张志英 | WUXI, JIANGSU

There are some fish you can eat head to tail, especially when they are as tiny as whitebait—also known as silver fish in Asian grocery stores. In China, you eat the whole thing, no problem. Nowadays, whitebait is considered an unsustainable fish because bigger fish feed on them, making these small fish essential to marine ecosystems. So to make this dish in the United States, a preferred substitute is sprat fish or cut strips from a trout fillet.

1 (1-pound) trout, cleaned, filleted, and cut into ½-inch slices

½ teaspoon freshly ground white pepper

2 teaspoons sea salt

4 tablespoons peanut oil

1 (1-inch) piece peeled fresh ginger, minced

2 tablespoons Shaoxing cooking wine or dry sherry

1 tablespoon soy sauce

1 scallion, finely chopped (green and white parts divided)

1 (2-inch) piece of carrot, slivered

5 eggs, beaten in a large bowl

In a large bowl, combine the fish, white pepper, and salt, and gently coat the fish with the seasoning. Set aside.

In a wok over medium-high heat, add 2 tablespoons of peanut oil and heat until shimmering. Add the ginger and stir-fry until fragrant, about 10 seconds. Add the fish and stir-fry for 2 minutes, keeping the fish pieces separated. Slowly stir in the cooking wine and the soy sauce. Add the white part of the scallion and the carrot, and stir-fry for 1 minute. Remove from heat, drain, and let cool on a plate for a few minutes. Add the stir-fried fish to the bowl of beaten egg, and toss gently to coat evenly.

Heat 1 tablespoon of peanut oil to the wok. Working in batches, add enough fish-egg mixture to make an omelet that you feel comfortable flipping. Reduce the heat to medium. When the omelet has set and it frees easily from the pan, 1 to 2 minutes, flip it and cook on the other side for 1 minute.

Remove the omelet from wok and cover loosely with foil to keep warm. Repeat the process until all the fish-egg mixture has been cooked, adding the remaining 1 tablespoon of oil as needed. Garnish with the scallion green parts and serve hot.

COOKING TIP: Omelets aren't always easy to make. Make an omelet the size you are comfortable with flipping. If you mess up, don't worry. This recipe is just as good scrambled.

FISH AND TOFU SOUP

Jì Yú Dòu Fu Tāng 鲫鱼豆腐汤

FAMILY: ZHANG ZHIYING 张志英 | WUXI, JIANGSU

This recipe makes a lovely fish soup for any time of year. It's light enough to enjoy in the summer, yet satisfying and warming in the cold season. The original recipe calls for carp, but striped bass or trout will offer the same rewards.

1 whole carp, striped bass, or trout (1½ pounds), cleaned, with head and tail intact

2 tablespoons Shaoxing cooking wine or dry sherry, divided

1 teaspoon sea salt

¼ cup peanut oil, plus 2 tablespoons

1 (1-inch) piece peeled fresh ginger, slivered

1 bunch enoki mushrooms (needle mushrooms)

8 ounces firm tofu, cut into 1-inch cubes

¼ cup dried shiitake mushrooms, soaked in ½ cup warm water for 5 minutes . (reserve the water)

1 tablespoon soy sauce

¼ teaspoon freshly ground white pepper

1 scallion, green part only, finely chopped

Cut 3 scores, ½ inch deep, across the side of the fish from top to bottom at the thickest part. In a small bowl, combine 1 tablespoon of wine and the salt, and rub it onto the fish, inside and out. Let the fish marinate while you prepare the rest of the dish.

In a wok over high heat, heat ¼ cup of peanut oil until shimmering. Add the fish, and fry for 2 minutes on each side, or until golden. Transfer the fish to a paper towel–lined plate to drain, and discard the oil. Rinse and wipe out the wok.

In the wok over medium-high heat, add the remaining 2 tablespoons of peanut oil. Add the ginger and stir-fry until fragrant, about 10 seconds. Add the enoki mushrooms, tofu, shiitake mushrooms and their soaking water, the soy sauce, and the remaining 1 tablespoon of wine. Stir-fry for 1 minute.

Add 3 cups of water and bring to a quick boil. Reduce the heat to medium and return the fish to the wok. Boil the fish for 5 minutes. Turn the fish over and boil for 5 minutes. Add the white pepper, and stir gently,

Transfer the dish to a serving bowl and garnish with the scallion.

VARIATION TIP: If a whole fish is inconvenient, feel free to use fillets.

INGREDIENT TIP: Enoki mushrooms can usually be found at Asian markets, Whole Foods, farmers' markets, and some grocery stores.

MUSSELS AND PORK RIB SOUP

Hé Bàng Xián Ròu Dòu Fu Bāo 河蚌咸肉豆腐煲

FAMILY: LU GUANGRONG 路广荣 | NANJING, JIANGSU

Nanjing, the former capital city of south China, undulates with hills and sunlight flickers through tree-lined streets. I met Sun Juan, a Chinese English teacher, in her home. I had asked her to teach me three dishes, but she and neighbor Lu Guangrong showed me 15 recipes instead! They wanted me to share Chinese cuisine with the rest of the world. This is my variation of a Nanjing specialty that showcases the irresistible flavor combination of seafood and pork. The original recipe used freshwater mussels that were enormous compared to the ones typically found in US markets. Lu Guangrong also removed the shells and boiled them until they were slightly tough. I've chosen to keep the shells on as it helps indicate when the mussels are perfectly cooked.

Special equipment: bamboo steamer or a wire rack for the wok

FOR THE PORK RIBS

¼ pound pork spare ribs, cut into 1-inch pieces

1 tablespoon Shaoxing cooking wine or dry sherry

2 teaspoons sea salt

¼ teaspoon sugar

¼ teaspoon freshly ground white pepper

1 tablespoon potato starch

FOR THE MUSSELS

5 pounds fresh mussels, soaked for 20 minutes

2 tablespoons peanut oil

3 scallions, chopped (white and green parts separated)

5 cloves garlic, sliced

2 tablespoons Shaoxing cooking wine or dry sherry

2 teaspoons sea salt, plus more as needed

1 (14-ounce) box of tofu, cut into 1-inch cubes

¼ teaspoon freshly ground white pepper

CONTINUED

TO MAKE THE PORK RIBS

In a medium bowl, combine the ribs, cooking wine, salt, sugar, and pepper, and mix until the ribs are coated. Cover and marinate for 30 minutes.

In a small bowl, combine the potato starch and 1 teaspoon of water, pour on the marinated ribs, and toss to mix.

In a wok over high heat, add 3 cups of water and bring to a boil. Place the ribs in a heatproof bowl and put the bowl into the steamer basket or onto a wire rack fitted for a wok. Steam for 10 minutes. Remove and set aside.

TO MAKE THE MUSSELS

Soak the mussels in a bucket of cold fresh water for at least 20 minutes or until you plan to cook them. After the mussels have soaked, put them in a large bowl in the sink and run them under cold water. If the mussels are farmed, they may already be debearded. To be sure, check for the beard or byssal thread. Hold the mussel in one hand. With the other, get a grip on the beard and pull it off, toward the hinge end of the mussel. When done, transfer the mussels into another bowl of clean, cold water. Clean the mussels of any sand or mud, and rinse. Dry them on a towel before cooking.

In the wok over high heat, heat the peanut oil until shimmering. Add the white parts of the scallion and the garlic, and stir-fry until fragrant, about 20 seconds. Add the mussels, cooking wine, salt, and 8 cups of water. Bring to a gentle boil for 3 minutes, then add the pork ribs and tofu. When the mussels start to open, stir gently for 2 minutes to help the soup flow into the open shells. Add the white pepper, and season with salt.

Transfer to a serving bowl. To serve, garnish with the scallion greens.

COOKING TIP: Mussels are usually sold and cooked alive. Discard any mussels with that have cracked, chipped, or gaping shells—they're no good. As soon as you bring the fresh mussels home, unwrap them to let them breathe. Discard any mussels that open before cooking, as well as any that don't open after cooking.

VARIATION TIP: Combining the flavors of seafood with pork creates a rich flavor. If you don't want to use pork ribs, try adding salt-cured pork or Chinese bacon.

STEAMED WHITEFISH

Zhēng Bái Yú 蒸白鱼

FAMILY: ZHANG ZHIYING 张志英 | WUXI, JIANGSU

This dish originally used the silvery Tai Lake whitefish, one of Tai Lake's "Three Whites" (white shrimp, whitebait, and whitefish). The fish is also known as Silver Sword. In the late Ming dynasty (1368 to 1644), a Tai Lake fisherman named Zhang San led the people to revolt against invading Qing soldiers. His arm was shot by an arrow, and the sword he was holding fell into the lake. As he stood in severe pain, soldiers rushed to attack him, but he managed to quickly bend down to fetch his sword in the lake and raise it to strike. The soldiers stopped in fear and ran away quickly. Surprised by their reaction, Zhang San soon realized that he was holding a silver fish and not a sword. Since then, "silver sword" has been a popular name for the fish.

Special equipment: bamboo steamers or a wire rack for the wok

1 whitefish, bass, or trout (2 pounds), cleaned

3 tablespoons Shaoxing cooking wine, divided

2 teaspoons sea salt

2 tablespoons soy sauce

½ teaspoon sugar

1 tablespoon sesame oil

1 (2-inch) piece peeled fresh ginger, julienned

1 scallion, julienned, pieces soaked in cold water to curl

Make 3 deep cuts (½ inch deep and 1 inch apart) across each side of the fish in the fat part. In a small bowl, mix 1 tablespoon of cooking wine with the salt, and rub it on the fish, inside and out. Place the fish on a large plate that will fit within a bamboo steamer or inside a wok on a rack.

In a wok over high heat, insert a wire rack into a wok, or use bamboo steam baskets, over 3 cups of water. Bring the water to a boil. Place the plated fish on the rack or in the basket and steam over high heat for 12 to 15 minutes.

While the fish steams, prepare the sauce. In a small saucepan, combine the remaining 2 tablespoons of cooking wine, the soy sauce, sugar, and sesame oil, and heat until the sugar dissolves.

Transfer the fish to an oval serving plate and pour the sauce over the fish. Garnish with the ginger and the scallion greens.

SERVING TIP: For extra color, add a few sprigs of cilantro and a sliced red chile pepper to the top of the fish.

CHAPTER EIGHT

TOFU & VEGETABLES

Dry-Cooked Green Beans (page 157)

CELERY WITH SMOKED TOFU

Xiāng Gān Chǎo Yě Qín 香干炒野芹

FAMILY: YANG AILIAN 杨爱连 | CHANGDE, HUNAN

Chinese celery is thinner than the stalks of celery found in Western markets. Like our celery, Chinese celery is crisp and full of water, but it is more aromatic and has a stronger flavor. Use the entire stalk with the leaves. If you don't have an Asian market nearby, see the Substitution Tip for a good stand-in. This dish is full of contrasting flavor from the celery and the smoked tofu. Smoked tofu is firm and its flavor comes from being smoked with tea leaves. If you can't find this kind of tofu, select tofu marinated in a Chinese five-spice blend, like Hodo Soy's Braised Tofu found at Whole Foods.

2 tablespoons peanut oil

7 ounces smoked tofu, cut into ¼-inch-thick matchsticks

1 teaspoon red pepper flakes or cayenne pepper

½ teaspoon sea salt

8 ounces Chinese celery, cut into 2-inch-long matchsticks

1 tablespoon chicken stock

In a wok over high heat, heat the peanut oil until it shimmers. Add the smoked tofu, red pepper flakes, and salt, and stir-fry for 3 minutes. Add the celery and stock, and stir-fry for 1 more minute.

Remove from heat and serve.

SUBSTITUTION TIP: Chinese celery can be found at Chinese or Asian grocers, but if you can't find it, cut Western celery into matchsticks and throw in a couple sprigs of cilantro cut to the same length.

STIR-FRIED CHINESE LONG BEANS WITH EGGPLANT

Jiāng Dòu Chǎo Qié Zi 豇豆炒茄子

FAMILY: LUO JIANHUA 罗建华 | CHANGSHA, HUNAN

This recipe creates a gorgeous vegetarian dish accented by the vibrant purple eggplant, green cowpeas (see Ingredient Tip), and red chiles. Chinese philosopher Confucius believed that dishes should be appealing to the eye, with a balance of color. This could be a dish the great sage would approve of, and it makes a beautiful addition to a family-style Chinese meal.

6 tablespoons peanut oil

1 tablespoon minced peeled fresh ginger

1 large Chinese eggplant, cut into ¼-inch matchsticks 2 inches long

6 fresh Chinese long beans or ¼ pound fresh green beans, cut into 2-inch pieces

½ cup pickled chile peppers (see page 21), finely chopped

1 tablespoon soy sauce

1 teaspoon sea salt

1 teaspoon sesame oil

In a wok over medium-high heat, heat the oil until it shimmers. Add the ginger and stir-fry until fragrant, about 10 seconds. Add the eggplant and long beans, and stir-fry for 3 to 4 minutes, or until the eggplant softens. Add the pickled chili peppers, soy sauce, and salt, and stir-fry for 2 minutes.

Taste a long bean—the dish is done when the flavors are blended well. Drizzle with the sesame oil and serve.

INGREDIENT TIP: The joy of Chinese eggplant is that it doesn't need to be peeled. And Chinese long beans are also known as yard-long beans, cowpeas, or long-podded cowpeas. They're found in Asian grocers, Whole Foods, and farmers' markets.

SUBSTITUTION TIP: Pickled chile peppers lend a savory and bright flavor to the dish, but if you can't find pickled red chiles from China, use pickled Thai bird's eye chiles. If neither is available, or if you simply prefer a milder flavor, use one red bell pepper to retain the balance of color for the dish.

CELTUCE WITH GARLIC CHIVES

Jiǔ Cài Chǎo Wō Sǔn 韭菜炒萵笋

FAMILY: ZHOU JUXIANG 周菊香 | CHANGSHA, HUNAN

Celtuce is also known as stem lettuce or Taiwanese lettuce. The possibilities for using this vegetable are endless: The leaves can be eaten raw in a salad or dipped in a sesame or sweet noodle sauce, or they can be cooked in a stir-fry with a little oil, garlic, and salt. This recipe features the stem, or rather the inner stem, which is tender and great for pickling or stir-frying. Garlic chives also play an important part in this dish. They look like scallions but taste more like garlic. You can often find them at your local farmers' market in season.

1 stalk celtuce or broccoli stem

1 large garlic chive or 1 scallion plus 1 clove garlic

2 tablespoons peanut oil

1 tablespoon chopped pickled chiles

2 tablespoons chicken stock

1 teaspoon sea salt, to taste

Peel the celtuce stalk until only the light green core remains. Cut the core into ¼-inch matchsticks, 2 inches long. In a medium saucepan, parboil for 8 minutes. Drain.

Cut the garlic chives into 2-inch-long pieces.

In a wok, heat the peanut oil over high heat until it shimmers. Add the pickled chiles, and stir-fry for 10 seconds. Add the celtuce and stir-fry for 1 minute. Add the stock and stir-fry until the liquid has almost evaporated, about 3 minutes. Add the garlic chive and stir-fry for 2 minutes.

Season with salt. Serve hot.

INGREDIENT TIP: You can find pickled chilies in an Asian grocery store. They may come whole or chopped. If you can't find pickled chiles, you can use fewer fresh chiles as the spice will be more intense. Add a splash of apple cider or white vinegar.

COMBINATION VEGETABLE SALAD

Dà Bàn Liáng Cài 大拌凉菜

FAMILY: FANG RUNHUA 方润花 | JINING, INNER MONGOLIA

This hydrating salad is full of big flavor and big crunch! In fact, "big" is how I might describe most things in Inner Mongolia. The three warm-smiling ayis who showed me how to cook it used big portions, as they were feeding my assistant Juling, my videographer Gregory, and me, plus other family members. When I looked around while standing in the middle of the plains, the sky was big! The land stretched out far. Big sights! The sheep that grazed on over 18 types of herbs in the grasslands—they too were big! This salad is a big dose of vegan goodness. You can find the soft crêpe paper–like tofu skin at Asian grocery stores.

FOR THE SALAD

1 pound Mung Bean Noodles (page 41)

2 large carrots

1 large cucumber

3½ ounces tofu skin

4 ounces mung bean sprouts with small leaves, blanched

1 small handful finely chopped cilantro leaves and stems

2 scallions, finely chopped

FOR THE DRESSING

2 tablespoons flaxseed oil

2 tablespoons rice wine vinegar

2 cloves garlic, minced

1 teaspoon ground ginger

1 teaspoon freshly ground Sichuan peppercorns

1 teaspoon sea salt

TO MAKE THE SALAD

Cut the noodles, carrots, cucumber, and tofu skin into ¼-inch matchsticks, matching the mung bean sprouts in shape and size. In a big salad bowl, spread out the noodles first, then layer the tofu skin, then the carrots, then the cucumber, and finally the bean sprouts. Top with the cilantro and scallion.

TO MAKE THE DRESSING

In a small bowl, add the flaxseed oil, vinegar, garlic, ginger, peppercorns, and salt. Whisk until well blended, and drizzle over the salad. Toss the salad just before serving to let the dressing marinate the noodles and tofu skin at the bottom.

VARIATION TIP: Test out some other vegetables for crunch like daikon, watermelon radish, or jicama. For tofu skin, you can also use bean curd sticks, but soak them in water for at least 8 hours or overnight before using.

FRIED GLUTEN BALLS STUFFED WITH BAMBOO SHOOTS AND MUSHROOMS

Chǎo Miàn Jin 炒面筋

FAMILY: QUAN HUIYING 全慧英 │ SHANGHAI

Growing up, I was not a fan of bamboo shoots because they were canned. It wasn't until I moved to China and had a stir-fry with fresh bamboo shoots that I realized what I had been missing. Fresh bamboo shoots have a light flavor and a crisp, smooth texture—and they take on the flavors of the recipe. They can be found at Asian grocers. Interestingly, my parents grew golden and black bamboo but never cooked it, and I still remember Laotian ladies passing by and asking my parents if they could harvest the shoots.

1 (8-ounce) fresh bamboo shoot

1 package fried gluten balls
(see Ingredient Tip)

1 teaspoon potato starch

2 tablespoons peanut oil

6 fresh shiitake mushrooms,
sliced ¼ inch thick

7 straw mushrooms,
sliced ¼ inch thick

1 medium king oyster
mushroom, sliced ¼ inch thick

1 teaspoon sea salt

Bring a pot of water to boil over high heat. Cut lengthwise along one side of the bamboo shoot, and peel away the tough outer leaves until you reach a tender inner stalk. Cut off the woody end. Put the shoot in the boiling water and simmer for 30 minutes, or until tender enough for a knife to easily pierce the surface. Remove from the heat and discard the water. When the bamboo shoot has cooled, slice it diagonally into ¼-inch-thick slices, 2 inches long.

Put 1 cup of cold water into a large bowl. Use your thumb to poke a hole into each fried gluten ball and put them in the water to soak for 5 minutes. Remove the wilted balls from the water, reserving ⅓ cup of water. In a small bowl, combine 1 tablespoon of water with the potato starch. Mix well to dissolve the starch.

In a wok, heat the peanut oil over high heat until it shimmers. Add the bamboo shoots, shiitake mushrooms, straw mushrooms, king oyster mushrooms, and salt, and stir-fry to mix. Add the reserved ⅓ cup water, and simmer for 3 minutes. Add the fried gluten balls and stir-fry for 2 minutes. Add the potato starch mixture and stir-fry for 1 minute.

Remove from heat and serve warm.

INGREDIENT TIP: Fried gluten balls are sold in packages in Asian markets and on Amazon.

VARIATION TIP: This dish can be as much about the mushrooms as the bamboo shoots. Try using other fresh mushrooms that are locally available.

NOT AN AYI

I can't call Chen Qiufan "Ayi," because she's around my age. Qiufan picked me up at the train station with a headache. She was the first native Chinese woman I met who admitted to liking wine. I was happy to find a kindred spirit. Just like me, she and her girlfriends go on trips to enjoy food and wine, taking a bus from Foshan to Macau to eat, drink, and bring a few bottles home.

From the train station, we stopped by an open-air market to buy some ingredients. As she wandered through the aisles concentrating on the menu, I saw her pass a stall selling snake. Across from that was a stall selling alligator. The poor animal was hacked in half and still alive with its mouth duct-taped shut. (In Guangdong, they say that they eat anything with its back to the sky.) I asked Qiufan if she knew how to cook snake, and she asked me if I wanted to learn. I said yes!

What I loved about the dishes Qiufan taught me were the flavors. Sand Ginger Steamed Chicken (page 94) has a flavor and fragrance I'd never experienced before but fell in love with for its nuttiness and simplicity. Who knew chicken could be cooked in a rice cooker and taste so good? Large fresh clams steamed with garlic and sesame oil, a minced blend of pork and cuttlefish, and even the snake stir-fried with leek blossoms and julienned bell peppers—all were so different, yet memorable for their fresh and vibrant flavors. In the case of snake, Qiufan tamed the fear that tainted my expectations and created a beautiful dish whose accompanying ingredients also felt like poetry.

Top to bottom: Chen Qiufan cooks before her myriad of sauces. The Chen family with Chen Zhigang (father), Chen Lu (daughter), and Chen Qiufan (mother and the cook). Sand Ginger Steamed Chicken easily made in a rice cooker.

CHINESE KALE WITH GINGER JUICE

Jiāng Jiǔ Chǎo Jiè Lán Piàn 姜酒炒芥兰片

FAMILY: CHEN QIUFAN 陈秋凡 | FOSHAN, GUANGDONG

This simple stir-fry of Chinese kale could be any old stir-fry, but Qiufan's creativity and gift for enticing with flavor adds the juice of ginger, whose heat softens the bitterness of the kale. A bit of ginger is often cooked with sturdy greens like kale—ginger is considered a warm food, which counteracts the cool properties of kale in Chinese herbal medicine.

1 pound Chinese kale

3 tablespoons fresh ginger juice

3 tablespoons peanut oil

2 cloves garlic, minced

½ teaspoon sea salt, plus more for seasoning

1 tablespoon Shaoxing cooking wine or dry sherry

Cut the Chinese kale into 1-inch strips. Using a garlic press or mortar and pestle, extract the juice from a ginger root until you have 3 tablespoons.

In a wok over medium-high heat, add the peanut oil and heat until it shimmers. Add the garlic and stir-fry until fragrant, about 10 seconds. Add the Chinese kale, ¼ cup of water, and salt, and simmer for 4 to 5 minutes or until the liquid has mostly evaporated. Add the ginger juice and the cooking wine. Stir-fry for 1 to 2 minutes, and season with salt.

Remove from heat and serve.

COOKING TIP: Wait until near the end of the cooking process to add the ginger juice, and be careful not to overcook it; otherwise, Qiufan says, it will become bitter.

STIR-FRIED BEAN SPROUTS

Rú Yì Cài 如意菜

FAMILY: XU WEIWEN 许伟文 | WUXI, JIANGSU

In the past, married women often wore hairpins called *ruyì*—a symbol of good fortune. Yellow bean sprouts look very similar to *ruyì*. As such, in Wuxi, it is customary to cook this dish during the Spring Festival to welcome good luck into the New Year. The dish is light in flavor with savory earthiness from the bean sprouts and soy sauce.

8 fried gluten balls

2 tablespoons peanut oil

1 pound mung bean sprouts

6 fresh shiitake mushrooms, diagonally sliced into small pieces

6 wood ear mushrooms, trimmed and torn into 1-inch pieces

4 ounces dried bamboo shoots, soaked overnight and cut into 2-inch pieces (see Ingredient Tip)

8 ounces smoked tofu, thinly sliced into 2-inch pieces

2 teaspoons sea salt

½ cup chicken or vegetable stock

2 tablespoons sesame oil

1 scallion, green part, chopped

Soak the fried gluten balls in water until soft, and then tear each into 4 pieces.

In a wok over medium-high heat, heat the peanut oil until it shimmers. Add the bean sprouts and stir-fry for 3 minutes. Add the shiitake mushrooms, wood ear mushrooms, and dried bamboo shoots, and stir-fry for 2 minutes.

Add the fried gluten ball pieces, smoked tofu, salt, and stock, and reduce the heat to low. Simmer for 2 minutes. Stir-fry for another 2 minutes or until the stock has mostly evaporated. Drizzle with the sesame oil and stir-fry for 1 minute.

Transfer to a serving plate and garnish with the chopped scallion greens.

INGREDIENT TIP: To prep the dried bamboo shoots, rinse them in water, then squeeze the shoots to remove the preservatives. Immerse them in a bowl of water and soak for at least 6 hours or overnight to make them pliable. Change the water when it becomes cloudy. Squeeze the shoots again and rinse thoroughly.

GOLDEN NEEDLE MUSHROOM SALAD

Jīn Zhēn Gū Liáng Bàn Cài 金针菇凉拌菜

FAMILY: GONG DONGHUA 龚冬华 | SHANGHAI

Golden needle mushrooms take their name from how they look—long and thin with a pearl-like cap. This dish surprised me with some of its Japanese influences when the mother in this Chinese family taught it to me. Gong Ayi used sweet Chinese sausage, which is popular in Cantonese cuisine, and the kicker for me was the wasabi oil. This dish is a lively side in a savory meal.

3 to 4 ounces enoki mushrooms, cleaned

1 Chinese sausage

1 small cucumber, julienned

1 tablespoon sesame oil

1 teaspoon soy sauce

¼ teaspoon sea salt

3 drops wasabi oil

Bring a pot of water to a boil over high heat. Add the enoki mushrooms and parboil them for 1 minute. Watch carefully, as they overcook easily. Use a slotted spoon to remove the mushrooms, and set aside on a plate to cool.

Return the water in the pot to a boil. Add the sausage and boil for 10 minutes. Transfer the sausage to a cutting board and discard the water. Slice the sausage into ¼-inch matchsticks.

In a medium mixing bowl, combine the mushrooms, sausage, cucumber, sesame oil, soy sauce, salt, and wasabi oil. Mix all ingredients well, then transfer to a serving dish.

Serve as a side dish.

SUBSTITUTION TIP: If you don't have wasabi oil, but still want the kick, use 1 teaspoon or more of Scorched Chili Oil (page 37) with sediment. It offsets the sweetness from the sausage with a little heat.

STIR-FRIED ADUKI BEANS WITH PICKLED MUSTARD GREENS

Suān Cài Chǎo Hóng Dòu 酸菜炒红豆

FAMILY: LIU MINGQIAN 刘明谦 | SUIJIANG, YUNNAN

When I learned this dish, my surprise at the inclusion of beans made me realize that I had preconceptions about what Chinese food was, and they were starting to crack. This dish is filled with goodness from the value-packed aduki beans to the gut-supportive pickled greens.

½ cup pickled mustard greens, chopped

2 tablespoons peanut oil

2 scallions, chopped (green and white parts separated)

1 (15.5-ounce can) aduki beans, drained and rinsed

¼ teaspoon sea salt

Heat a wok over high heat, and dry-fry the pickled mustard greens to remove their liquid. Transfer to a plate and set aside. Rinse and dry the wok.

In the wok, heat the peanut oil over medium-high heat until it shimmers. Add the chopped white scallion parts and stir-fry until fragrant, about 20 seconds. Add the beans and stir-fry for 2 minutes. Add the pickled mustard greens and continue to stir-fry until all the flavors have blended well, about 2 minutes. Add the scallion greens and stir-fry, about 1 minute. Add the salt and stir to mix.

Transfer to a plate and serve.

VARIATION TIP: Add a little heat (or a lot) by adding two dried chile peppers snapped in two into the oil with the scallions, before adding the beans.

SPINACH BUNDLES WITH SESAME SAUCE

Zhī Má Jiàng Bō Cài 芝麻醬菠菜

FAMILY: XIAO XIA 肖霞 | CHENGDU, SICHUAN

The mother who taught me this recipe was crafty at finding ways to feed her two boys healthy food, and that meant making even the least favorable veggies likeable. I would guess this recipe will help spinach-haters of all ages happily eat this leafy green.

1 tablespoon tahini (sesame paste)

3 tablespoons toasted sesame seeds

2 tablespoons sea salt

4 ounces young spinach leaves, root tips still intact, if possible, to hold the leaves together while blanching

In a small bowl, add the tahini, and slowly stir in water until the sauce has a runny consistency. In another small bowl, add the toasted sesame seeds.

Bring a pot of water to boil over high heat and add the salt. Blanch the spinach, but take care not to overcook it; it cooks quickly. Remove the spinach immediately from the heat (makes quick work with a slotted spoon if using loose spinach) and plunge into cold water. Remove the root tips.

Separate the spinach into several bundles. Drain and squeeze the water from the cut spinach carefully. Gently squeeze the soft spinach into ropes. Cut the spinach rope into 2-inch bundles. Dip one side of each spinach bundle into the tahini then dip the sauced end into the bowl of toasted sesame seeds. Set the spinach bundle on its side on a serving plate. Repeat with the remaining spinach bundles.

SUBSTITUTION TIP: You can find tahini (sesame paste) in an Asian grocery, and many supermarkets carry it. If you can't find either, use a smooth unsweetened natural peanut butter.

MUSHROOM MARKET TO TABLE

Eager with anticipation for another culinary adventure, I rode a bus from Kunming through lush green hillsides terraced with rice paddies and featuring new developments that could have been stucco homes in Anytown, USA. As I stepped off the bus into dry heat, I was caught by dust-filled air from construction nearby. Across the dry clay–caked road, I spotted a horse standing in the hot sun with its muzzle attached to a feed bag—like all of us, eat it must.

I arrived at the house of the Li family—the mother, Zhang Ayi, retired from the State Forestry Administration; her husband Li Shifu, who still works with the Grain Bureau; and their son, Li Jianhui, who studies design. After setting my backpack down, Zhang Ayi smiled warmly, scooted us right back out the door, and walked down the street to a market, prefacing our cooking with an outing to discover the mushrooms of Wudìng.

A lady, grinning with perfectly aligned teeth, approached us with a basket of mushrooms, her finds from foraging in the mountains. The mushrooms were as large as portobellos with stems as long as carrots. I would learn that they are called termite mushrooms or *Termitomyces albuminosus* (and yes, these mushrooms are in fact grown with the help of termites, who carry and drop their seeds and fertilize them with their manure!).

As we turned onto another road, farmers and foragers lined the curb, and at their feet sat vibrant-colored mushrooms that left me in awe. Apparently, many comb through the mountains harvesting the mushrooms as they come into season. And here on Wukang Street, they gather to sell their wild-found harvests at this magical mushroom market.

Many of the mushrooms in the market can only be found in Yunnan. A great deal are exported to Japan frozen or dried, but true joy is to have them fresh. I found myself living a rare and fortunate moment.

We returned home with a few types of mushrooms, and Zhang Ayi began preparing our meal. I remember thinking with pleasure, "She hasn't stopped smiling since we arrived." Visually impressive even prior to cooking, once sliced the porcini mushrooms revealed watercolor hues of blues and greens. I learned that as it cooks, the

Clockwise: Zhang Ayi and her son Li Jianhui shop for their meal. Local farmer at Wukang Road's mushroom market in Wuding. Zhang Ayi holding a termite mushroom (Jizong mushroom).

color mellows, but what the porcini loses in color, it retains in flavor. She quickly fried the porcini with dried chiles, garlic, and 6 tablespoons of the special ingredient: smoked Yunnan lard. Zhang Ayi's porcini mushroom stir-fried with chiles is irresistible in taste and toothy texture, as replicated in Stir-Fried Porcini Mushrooms and Dried Chiles (page 152).

Meanwhile, Zhang Ayi painstakingly tore some *Thelephora ganbajun* mushrooms into thumbnail-sized pieces and sliced spicy red chiles. She stir-fried both with walnut oil. This variety of mushroom had a smoked, woody flavor.

The table was set with other savory fixings, including Mashed Edamame (page 153), smoked bacon fried rice, smoked air-dried bacon, broad beans, kidney beans stewed with smoked bacon, and a side of the sliced smoked bacon again, but this time fried. Yes, there was a definite theme here. The nutritional upside of this meal was beans and mushrooms; they are very healthy. However, they become less beneficial when fried with cured pork and lard.

"Farmers and foragers lined the curb and at their feet sat vibrant-colored mushrooms that left me in awe."

Either way, I wasn't complaining, as I was in culinary heaven. The flavors fit well among my favorites, and Zhang Ayi's infectious smile, paired with the comforts of pork, mushrooms, and beans, lent the cozy feeling of home that had been missing.

As a parting gift, Zhang Ayi gave me a large jar of deep-fried termite mushrooms. When I brought this jar of mushrooms to share with my friends in Beijing, it felt like I had awakened from a wonderful dream but had proof that it was real.

Top to bottom: Zhang Ayi slicing fresh porcini mushrooms with a cleaver. The Li Family including Li Jianhui (son), Zhang Lijuan (mother and the cook), and Li Qiang (father).

STIR-FRIED PORCINI MUSHROOMS WITH DRIED CHILES

Gàn Jiāo Chǎo Niú Gān Jùn 干椒炒牛肝菌

FAMILY: ZHANG LIJUAN 张丽娟 | WUDING, YUNNAN

I learned this recipe in the "shroomy" province of China, Yunnan. Walking through the daily market in Wuding, Yunnan, I observed many folks selling gorgeous mushrooms they had foraged from the forest. They weren't crimini or button types, but instead the sort you'd pay dearly for in gourmet markets. The fresh porcini showcased in this dish are a treat; they are wonderfully nutty in flavor with sturdy bottoms. When cleaning, use a sharp paring knife to lightly shave the woody ends. Use a paper towel to rub off any dirt from the caps and stems.

1 pound fresh porcini mushrooms

2 tablespoons Chinese bacon drippings or peanut oil

3 or 4 dried red chiles, snapped in two

3 cloves garlic, sliced

Sea salt

Cut the porcini into ¼-inch slices from the cap down to the stem, so you end up with silhouettes of the mushroom.

In a wok over high heat, add the bacon drippings and heat until sizzling. Reduce the heat to medium-high, and add the chiles and garlic. Stir-fry for 10 seconds, then add the porcini and gently stir-fry for 5 to 7 minutes, lifting them to keep them from sticking.

Season with salt and serve immediately.

INGREDIENT TIP: If you don't have fresh ones, you can reconstitute dried porcini in warm water for 15 to 20 minutes. Drain and set aside. Save the water in an airtight container in the refrigerator—it's great for enriching stocks and other dishes.

MASHED EDAMAME

Dòu Shēng 豆生

FAMILY: ZHANG LIJUAN 张丽娟 | WUDING, YUNNAN

This dish isn't pretty, but it is tasty and one of my favorites. If you like mashed potatoes with gravy, you've got to give this a try, and don't shy away from the bacon drippings—the small amount contributes big flavor. In fact, the Chinese name for this dish is "healthy beans" because of its nutrient-abundant soybeans. But you can make this dish healthier, and vegetarian, by simply leaving out the bacon drippings.

1 pound edamame, shelled

1 teaspoon sea salt

1 tablespoon walnut oil or peanut oil

1 tablespoon Chinese bacon drippings (or any bacon drippings)

1 teaspoon Sichuan peppercorns

1 stalk celery, finely chopped

1 spicy green chile such as serrano or jalapeño, finely chopped

Put the edamame in a pot with just enough water to cover the beans. Add the salt and bring to a boil over high heat, then reduce the heat to low and simmer for 15 minutes, or until the beans are soft. Remove from heat and purée the beans in a blender.

In a wok over high heat, heat the walnut oil and bacon drippings. Add the Sichuan peppercorns and fry until fragrant, about 15 seconds. Using a slotted spoon, remove the peppercorns and discard. Add the celery and chile pepper, and stir-fry for 2 minutes. Add the puréed edamame and mix well.

Season with salt and serve hot.

INGREDIENT TIP: The best way to get bacon drippings is to save them when you cook bacon and store in a lidded container. If you use Chinese bacon, simply slice it and bake it in the oven until cooked to perfection.

SUBSTITUTION TIP: If you don't want to use bacon drippings, 1 tablespoon of miso paste is another way to achieve an umami flavor for this dish.

STIR-FRIED CHINESE CABBAGE WITH RED CHILE

Chǎo Bái Cài 炒白菜

FAMILY: ZHANG LIN 张林 | SUIJIANG, YUNNAN

Here's proof that something so simple can also be so delicious. Napa cabbage is *the* cabbage in China. This stir-fry is easy, but carries in its flavor a depth of sweetness from the cabbage-garlic blend, and a tingling kick from the chile.

1 tablespoon peanut oil

3 cloves garlic, smacked and minced

1 fresh red chile such as red serrano, thinly sliced

1 pound napa cabbage, cut into 2-inch pieces

2 tablespoons chicken stock or water

Sea salt

In a wok over medium-high heat, heat the peanut oil until it shimmers. Stir-fry the garlic and chile pepper until fragrant, about 15 seconds.

Add the cabbage and stir-fry for 3 minutes. Add the stock and continue to stir-fry for 2 to 3 minutes, or until the cabbage is tender but not soggy.

Season with salt and serve.

SUBSTITUTION TIP: A fresh red chile may be too spicy for you or sometimes you just don't have one. If you have dried chiles in your pantry, use 1 or 2 of your favorite, snapping them in two before adding to the wok. You can also throw in a teaspoon of Sichuan peppercorns for added zing.

"TWO ACRES OF LAND"

Liǎng Mǔ Dì 两亩地

FAMILY: YANG XUKUN 杨旭昆	KUNMING, YUNNAN

The image-evoking name refers to the main ingredients: green soybean and corn. Each ingredient symbolizes one acre. My host and teacher of this dish, Yang Shifu, explained why the term "two acres of land" has auspicious meaning. Traditionally, the Chinese have been peasants. At least two acres of land were needed to support a family. However, many families could barely afford two acres, so they expressed their wishes through the phrase "two acres of land." Corn and beans were the most common crops, so people gave this dish a lucky name to attract good fortune. Yang Shìfu likes this dish because of its meaning and because it's healthy. When he cooked it for me, he emphasized that the vegetables he was using were organic. So if you can, by all means do the same!

1 pound edamame, shelled

1 pound corn kernels cut from fresh ears of corn

1 green bell pepper, finely chopped

1 red bell pepper, finely chopped

2 tablespoons peanut oil

Sea salt

If you use freshly shelled edamame, blanch for 5 minutes. If they are frozen, defrost them.

In a wok, heat the peanut oil over medium-high heat until it shimmers. Add the edamame, corn, green bell pepper, and red bell pepper, and stir-fry for 2 minutes. Season with salt.

Transfer to a serving dish and serve hot.

INGREDIENT TIP: When Yang Shifu taught me this dish, he used fresh ingredients. Alternately, you can buy frozen shelled edamame, which comes preblanched.

STEWED KALE

Yǔ Yī Gān Lán 焖羽衣甘蓝

Stewing tough greens like kale provides an easy and delicious way to add this hearty veggie to any meal. The dish is a great accompaniment to Red-Cooked Pork Shanghai Style (page 117).

1 pound Chinese kale

2 teaspoons fermented black beans

1 (1-inch) piece peeled fresh ginger, minced

2 cloves garlic, minced

1 tablespoon peanut oil

1 tablespoon soy sauce

1 tablespoon Shaoxing cooking wine or dry sherry

¼ teaspoon sugar

¼ cup chicken stock

Sea salt

1 tablespoon sesame oil

Wash the kale and cut it into 1-inch strips. Soak the fermented black beans in a small bowl for 5 minutes, and drain.

In a small bowl, combine the ginger, garlic, and fermented black beans, and mash together into a paste.

In a wok, heat the peanut oil over high heat until it shimmers. Add the ginger mixture and stir-fry until fragrant, about 10 seconds. Add the kale and stir-fry for 3 minutes. Add the soy sauce, cooking wine, sugar, and stock, and stir-fry for a few seconds just to mix.

Reduce the heat to low and simmer for 8 minutes, or until the kale leaves are tender. Season with salt, and drizzle with sesame oil. Serve hot.

VARIATION TIP: What green leaves are in season in your area? Don't feel restricted to Chinese kale; this recipe works beautifully with all kale and chard. Now that you have the flavorings, apply them to other greens for something different.

DRY-COOKED GREEN BEANS

Gān Biān Sì Jì Dòu 干煸四季豆

FAMILY: JIANG YI 蒋毅 | CHENGDU, SICHUAN

This dish is popular in China. It exemplifies how meat can be used as a flavoring for vegetables. You can use as little or as much pork as you wish. Pork isn't the hero in this dish, but it plays a significant supporting role.

3 tablespoons peanut oil, divided

½ pound green beans, ends and strings removed (if necessary), cut into 2-inch pieces

2 to 4 ounces ground fatty pork

1 (1-inch) piece peeled fresh ginger, minced

1 clove garlic, minced

2 teaspoons chili bean paste

½ teaspoon sea salt

In a wok over high heat, heat 1 tablespoon of peanut oil until it shimmers. Add the green beans. Stir-fry until they start to blister on all sides. Remove from heat and set aside on a plate.

Heat 1 tablespoon of oil in the wok and add the pork. Stir-fry to loosen up the meat, then push it to the side of the wok. Add the remaining 1 tablespoon of oil. Add the ginger, garlic, and chili bean paste, and stir-fry until fiery red and fragrant. Return the green beans to the wok and stir-fry to combine the pork and the green beans. Add the salt and stir-fry for 1 minute.

Serve hot.

VARIATION TIP: For a vegetarian version of this dish, you can omit the meat and add 1 tablespoon of dark soy sauce for umami.

RICE & NOODLES

Ants Climbing Tree (page 164)

EGG FRIED RICE, PLAIN AND SIMPLE

Dàn Chǎo Fàn 蛋炒饭

FAMILY: HAN XIANMING 韩先明 | BEIJING

The first and only rule of fried rice: Use cold rice. I like to cook more rice than I need for dinner and then keep the leftovers in the refrigerator for a morning fry-up. Cold rice is drier and less likely to clump in the wok. It's also easier to mash with the spatula to loosen the grains when it's cold. If rice is warm or hot, the grains stubbornly mash together—so why fight it? Make it plain and simple!

3 cups cooked rice, cold (preferably cooked the day before)

1 tablespoon soy sauce

½ teaspoon sea salt

¼ teaspoon sugar

¼ teaspoon freshly ground white pepper

2 tablespoons peanut oil

2 eggs, beaten

1 scallion, finely chopped

2 teaspoons sesame oil

In a large bowl, use your hands to loosen and crumble the cold rice. Add the soy sauce, salt, sugar, and pepper. Still using your hands, continue to loosen the rice while mixing it with the seasonings.

In a wok over high heat, heat the peanut oil until it shimmers. When it starts to smoke, add the eggs and stir-fry until they become a runny scramble. Add the seasoned rice and stir-fry for 2 to 3 minutes, or until the rice looks mostly dry of its sauce. Toss in the scallion and stir-fry for 1 or 2 minutes, then remove from heat.

Drizzle with sesame oil, and serve.

VARIATION TIP: For vegetable fried rice, you can use finely chopped Chinese kale stems, peas, and diced carrots. Add the vegetables after the egg, but before the rice.

LAMB FRIED RICE XINJIANG STYLE

Zi Rán Yáng Ròu Chǎo Fàn 孜然羊肉炒饭

I believe that one of the most transformative spices in the world is cumin. It's the Midas of spices—whatever it touches becomes irresistible. Before I started to cook Chinese food, I traveled to Urumqi and Kashgar in Xinjiang, the northwestern province of China that borders Tajikistan and Kyrgyzstan. I remember there was a rice dish that I could not get enough of—a pilaf of sorts called *polo*. Men standing by huge woks used large spatulas to stir-fry rice with cumin-seasoned carrots and the drippings of roasted lamb chops. This dish transports the senses.

FOR THE LAMB

1 pound lamb loin chops

1 tablespoon Shaoxing cooking wine or dry sherry

1 tablespoon soy sauce

2 teaspoons ground cumin

3 cloves garlic, minced

1 teaspoon minced peeled fresh ginger

1 teaspoon potato starch

½ teaspoon sea salt

FOR THE STIR-FRY

3 cups cooked rice, cold (preferably cooked the day before)

1 teaspoon sea salt, plus more as needed

¼ teaspoon freshly ground white pepper

2 tablespoons peanut oil

2 cloves garlic, minced

1 carrot, diced

1 tablespoon sesame oil, plus more for garnish

2 teaspoons dark soy sauce

1 scallion, finely chopped

TO MAKE THE LAMB

Cut the meat off the lamb chop and dice. Reserve the bone. In a medium bowl, add the lamb, bone, cooking wine, soy sauce, cumin, garlic, ginger, potato starch, and salt. Stir to mix well. Set aside for 10 minutes.

TO MAKE THE STIR-FRY

In a large bowl, use your hands to loosen the rice grains. Add the salt and pepper, and gently mix the rice, taking care to not smash the grains.

In a wok over high heat, heat the peanut oil until it shimmers. Add the garlic and stir-fry until fragrant, about 10 seconds. Add the lamb (with the bone) and stir-fry for 4 to 5 minutes. Add the carrot and stir-fry for 2 minutes. Add the rice and 1 tablespoon of sesame oil, and stir-fry for 2 minutes. Add the dark soy sauce and continue to stir-fry. Season with salt.

Drizzle with a little more sesame oil, and scatter the scallion on top. Serve hot.

SERVING TIP: Serve with Scorched Chili Oil (page 37) on the side.

MUNG BEAN NOODLES WITH SPICY SICHUAN SAUCE

Sìchuān Liáng Fěn 四川凉粉

One of my favorite dishes to eat at a Sichuan restaurant is *liang fen*—mung bean noodles topped with an addictively delicious sauce of chile and fermented black beans. The following recipe is based on intrinsic Sichuan flavors, and my own adaptation of the dish. Serve this cold dish at the beginning of a meal to whet the appetite.

1 tablespoon fermented black beans

14 ounces Mung Bean Noodles (page 41)

3 tablespoons Scorched Chili Oil with sediment (page 37)

2 tablespoons peanut oil

1 tablespoon sesame oil

1 tablespoon dark soy sauce

1 tablespoon Chinese black vinegar or balsamic vinegar

1 large clove garlic, minced

¼ teaspoon sugar

¼ teaspoon freshly ground Sichuan peppercorns

Sea salt

1 red serrano chile, thinly sliced

1 scallion, green part, finely chopped

Soak the fermented black beans in warm water for 5 minutes in a small bowl.

Rinse and cut the Mung Bean Noodles into shorter pieces for picking up more easily with chopsticks.

In a food processor or blender, put the black beans, scorched chili oil, peanut oil, 2 tablespoons of water, sesame oil, dark soy sauce, vinegar, garlic, sugar, and ground Sichuan peppercorns. Pulse the mixture until it becomes a smooth sauce. Season with salt.

Drizzle the sauce over the noodles. Garnish with the red chile and the scallion greens.

SUBSTITUTION TIP: In a pinch, if you don't have Mung Bean Noodles, use a block of soft tofu.

RICE NOODLES WITH PORK AND CHILES

Chǎo Hé Fěn 炒河粉

FAMILY: ZHANG XINYU 张欣雨 | CHENGDU, SICHUAN

As a kid, I loved *chao fen*. Now my son—a noodle monster like his mother—enjoys tagging along on the experience whenever I have a craving. You can use wide or thin noodles. In my opinion, the wider, the better.

8 ounces rice stick noodles, wide or thin

FOR THE PORK

2 teaspoons dark soy sauce

2 teaspoons Shaoxing cooking wine or dry sherry

1 teaspoon sesame oil

1 clove garlic, minced

¼ teaspoon potato starch

¼ teaspoon sea salt

¼ teaspoon freshly ground white pepper

8 ounces lean pork tenderloin, cut into ¼ inch strips

FOR THE STIR-FRY

3 tablespoons peanut oil

2 cloves garlic, sliced

1 tablespoon chili bean paste

1 red bell pepper, julienned

2 green chiles such as serrano or jalapeño, sliced

1 stalk celery, diagonally sliced

3 tablespoons dark soy sauce

2 teaspoons Chinkiang vinegar or balsamic vinegar

Sea salt

In a large bowl, soak the rice noodles in warm water for 20 minutes or until soft. Drain and set aside.

TO MAKE THE PORK

In a medium bowl, combine the dark soy sauce, cooking wine, sesame oil, garlic, potato starch, salt, white pepper, and the pork slices. Marinate for 15 minutes.

TO MAKE THE STIR-FRY

In a wok over high heat, heat the peanut oil until it shimmers. Stir-fry the marinated pork and its sauce for 3 minutes. Add the garlic, chili bean paste, red bell pepper, green chiles, and celery, and stir-fry for 1 minute. Add the rice noodles and stir in the dark soy sauce and vinegar. Stir-fry until all the flavors have blended.

Season with salt, and serve warm.

COOKING TIP: To slice the pork more easily, place the meat in the freezer for 15 minutes to firm it. Use a sharp knife to slice the pork as thinly as possible. After draining the boiled noodles, add 1 teaspoon of sesame oil to keep the noodles from sticking while they cool. They will also be easier to stir-fry.

ANTS CLIMBING TREE

Mǎ Yǐ Shàng Shù 蚂蚁上树

FAMILY: XIAO XIA 肖霞 | CHENGDU, SICHUAN

There is a story about a man by the name of Dou who was in a load of debt. He sold his daughter, Dou E, to his creditor, Cai Popo, as a child wife for her son. Dou E's husband soon passed away, and she was left to provide for her mother-in-law, which she proceeded to do through begging. One day she persuaded a vendor to give her a small chunk of pork and a handful of stick noodles. As she cooked the dish, her mother-in-law popped into the kitchen and asked what the delicious aroma was. Dou E replied, "It's stir-fried stick noodle!" When she served the dish to Cai Popo, her mother-in-law asked, "Why are there many ants?" Dou E explained they were bits of meat from the morsel she obtained to feed them. Her mother-in-law was touched, and with humor said, "Let's call this dish 'Ants Climbing the Tree!' "

4 ounces rice stick noodles

1 teaspoon sesame oil

2 tablespoons peanut oil, divided

1 teaspoon peeled fresh ginger, minced

1 teaspoon garlic, minced

2 teaspoons chili bean paste

4 ounces ground lean pork

¼ teaspoon freshly ground black pepper

1 teaspoon Shaoxing cooking wine or dry sherry

1 teaspoon soy sauce

1 teaspoon dark soy sauce

½ teaspoon sugar

1 cup chicken stock

Sea salt

1 teaspoon red bell pepper, finely chopped

1 scallion, green part, finely chopped

Soak the rice noodles in a large bowl of warm water for 15 minutes, or until soft. Drain the noodles and toss with the sesame oil to keep separated. Discard the water.

In a wok over high heat, heat the peanut oil until shimmering. Add the ginger and garlic, and stir-fry until fragrant, about 10 seconds. Add the chili bean paste and stir-fry until fiery and blended, about 1 minute.

Add the ground pork and stir-fry until it separates into bits. Add the pepper, cooking wine, soy sauce, dark soy sauce, sugar, and stock, and bring to a simmer. Add the noodles and stir occasionally until most of the stock has evaporated. Season with salt.

Garnish with the red bell pepper and scallion greens.

VARIATION TIP: This dish needs very little meat, as told in the story of Dou E. You can also use ground chicken, ground beef, or for a vegetarian version, crumbled tofu.

VARIATION TIP: Ants Climbing Tree is typically made with thin-stick noodles, but using wide-stick noodles doesn't change the flavor. Personally, I find the fatter noodles to be more fun—and my son agrees.

CAT'S EAR PASTA

Māo Ěr Duǒ 猫耳朵

FAMILY: FANG RUNHUA 方润花 | JINING, INNER MONGOLIA

This hearty pasta keeps the belly full in Inner Mongolia. The pasta itself is named for its resemblance to cat ears, a shape that helps carry the sauce in every bite. This dish makes a great one-pot meal that will fill the family.

4 ounces orecchiette

8 ounces potatoes, diced

1 medium carrot, diced

2 tablespoons flaxseed oil

1 teaspoon Sichuan peppercorns

1 whole star anise

1 teaspoon ginger powder

1 scallion, finely chopped

4 ounces tomato, diced

8 ounces white onion, diced

6 ounces green bell pepper, diced

2 cloves garlic, sliced

Sea salt

1 tablespoon dark soy sauce

Bring a medium pot of water to a boil over over high heat and cook the pasta for 4 to 5 minutes. Drain, and cool under cold water. Drain and set aside.

Bring a large pot of water to a boil. Add the potatoes and carrot, and cook for 3 minutes. Remove from the heat, drain, and set aside.

In a wok over high heat, heat the flaxseed oil until it shimmers. Add the peppercorns and star anise, and stir-fry until fragrant, about 10 seconds. Use a slotted spoon to remove the peppercorns and discard them. Add the ginger powder and scallion, and stir-fry for 1 minute. Add the tomatoes, onion, green bell pepper, and garlic, and stir-fry until the tomatoes start to soften, 1 to 2 minutes. Season with salt. Add the pasta, potatoes, and carrot to the wok. Add the dark soy sauce and stir-fry until all the flavors have blended well.

Serve hot in bowls.

SERVING TIP: Serve with condiments of Scorched Chili Oil (page 37) and chopped scallion on the side.

SHEPHERD'S PURSE AND RICE CAKES

Jì Cài Chǎo Nián Gāo 荠菜炒年糕

FAMILY: XU WEIWEN 许伟文 | WUXI, JIANGSU

This dish is very simple in flavor and a specialty in the coastal province of Jiangsu. The Chinese name for sticky rice cakes is *nian gao*, which means "year cake." It's typically served to ring in the New Year. Shepherd's purse sounds fancier than it actually is; it's a wild plant that can sometimes be found at farmers' markets in the United States. Otherwise, you can find it frozen in an Asian grocery.

1 pound dried sticky rice cakes (rice ovalettes), soaked overnight in water at room temperature

8 ounces shepherd's purse, rinsed

2 tablespoons peanut oil

½ cup chicken stock

1 teaspoon soy sauce

1 tablespoon sesame oil

½ teaspoon sugar

Sea salt

Drain the rice cakes and discard the water. If using frozen shepherd's purse, rinse the greens a few times. Drain, then squeeze out excess water and chop well.

In a wok, heat the peanut oil over high heat until it shimmers. Add the rice cakes and stir-fry for 3 minutes, or until they start to blister. Add the stock and continue to stir-fry until the rice cakes become soft. Add the shepherd's purse, soy sauce, sesame oil, and sugar. Season with salt, then stir-fry until the flavors are well blended.

Serve warm.

SUBSTITUTION TIP: Shepherd's purse can be found in Asian grocers like Ranch 99 (see Resources, page 174). If you can't find shepherd's purse, you can use edible chrysanthemum leaves or spinach.

COOKING TIP: Take care not to overcook the rice cakes or they will start to stick to each other.

COLD MIXED NOODLES

Liáng Bàn Hóng Shǔ Fěn Sī 凉拌红薯粉丝

FAMILY: JIANG YI 蒋毅 | CHENGDU, SICHUAN

Jiang Yi was into explosive flavors. We were in Sichuan after all, where something's amiss if any dish in a meal is bland. While Jiang Yi and his sister cooked an entire menagerie in their kitchen, these noodles offered a vibrant vegetarian pause between the wriggling eels, scuttling crayfish, peppered pork, and Spicy Poached Beef Slices (page 100).

3 ounces dried sweet potato noodles

1 teaspoon sesame oil

1 scallion, finely chopped, plus 1 teaspoon minced, for garnish

2 cloves garlic, smacked and minced

2 teaspoons minced peeled fresh ginger

2 pickled chile peppers, minced

1 tablespoon soy sauce

1 teaspoon juice from pickled chile peppers in a jar

1 teaspoon garlic chili sauce

1 teaspoon sugar

1 teaspoon vinegar

1 teaspoon Shaoxing cooking wine or dry sherry

1 teaspoon Sichuan peppercorn oil

1 teaspoon sea salt, plus more as needed

Prepare a bowl of ice water. Cook the sweet potato noodles according to package. Drain and plunge them into the ice water bath for 4 minutes. Drain and toss with the sesame oil to prevent sticking. While preparing the rest of the dish, toss the noodles occasionally to reduce sticking.

In a large bowl, combine the scallion, garlic, ginger, chile peppers, soy sauce, chile pepper juice, garlic chili sauce, sugar, vinegar, cooking wine, and Sichuan peppercorn oil. Season with salt. Add the noodles, and toss to coat evenly.

You can chill these noodles while preparing the rest of your meal, or serve immediately. Garnish with the minced scallion before serving.

COOKING TIP: Sichuan peppercorn oil can be found at Asian markets. You can also make your own by seasoning hot oil in a wok with 3 tablespoons of Sichuan peppercorns.

SUBSTITUTION TIP: You can use any noodle that can be eaten cold. Try shirataki or rice vermicelli.

BEIJING-STYLE NOODLES

Lǎo Běijing Zhá Jiàng Miàn 老北京炸醬麵

Every family has their own style when making these noodles. The sauce is earthy yet sweet, and it freezes well for when you need a quick family meal during the week. When Peikwen, my fiancé at the time of my Chinese travels, was a child, his mother used to make her version of *zha jiang mian* and called it Chinese spaghetti. While Peikwen and I lived in Beijing, we explored the city a lot on bicycle, taxi, and even motor scooters (when we dared ride them without licenses), always searching for the noodle shop that could replicate his mother's recipe. But after six years of living in Beijing, we never found it. This is a noodle recipe I've adapted from original ones passed on to me by others. Like all recipes we cook again and again, I've made it my own—sweet, spicy, and influenced by my life in Beijing.

1 teaspoon sea salt

1 pound Handmade Noodles (page 43)

1 tablespoon sesame oil

1 tablespoon peanut oil

2 scallions, finely chopped

1 tablespoon minced peeled fresh ginger

3 cloves garlic, minced

1 pound pork belly, minced

2 tablespoons sweet noodle sauce

2 tablespoon chili bean paste

1 tablespoon dark soy sauce

1 tablespoon Shaoxing cooking wine or dry sherry

½ teaspoon sugar

1 cup chicken stock

Sea salt

1 cucumber, julienned

3 ounces watermelon radish, peeled, julienned

¼ cup chopped scallion

Bean sprouts (optional)

Bring a pot of water and the salt to a boil over high heat. Add the noodles and boil for 3 to 4 minutes. Remove from heat, drain, and rinse in cold water. Put them in a large bowl and toss with the sesame oil. Set aside.

Bring another pot of water to a boil, and keep it simmering while you prepare the sauce.

Heat the peanut oil in a wok over high heat. Add the scallions, ginger, and garlic, and stir-fry until fragrant, about 15 seconds. Add the minced pork belly and stir-fry until it starts to turn golden. Add the sweet noodle sauce, chili bean paste, dark soy sauce, cooking wine, sugar, and stock. Gently bring the mixture to a boil, reduce the heat to low, and simmer for 8 minutes. Over low heat, keep the sauce warm while you serve each person.

Using a spider, lower an individual serving of noodles into the pot of boiling water for 20 seconds, then raise and transfer the noodles to a small bowl. Pour sauce over the noodles and garnish with some of the cucumber, watermelon radish, scallion, and bean sprouts (if using). Repeat to make enough servings for all those at the table.

COOKING TIP: Some varieties of cucumber have tougher skins; these should be peeled. There's no need to peel hothouse or Persian cucumbers.

SERVING TIP: Chili bean paste packs heat, but it isn't really spicy. To spice this dish up, serve your guests Scorched Chili Oil (page 37) as a condiment. You can also serve the garnishes on the side and let each guest choose for themselves how they'd like to enjoy their noodles.

ACKNOWLEDGMENTS

Thank you **Mom and Dad** for your stories that gave me the hunger to find my own. The courage you both possessed in crossing borders (figuratively and literally) and keeping an open mind is not easy to find, but it has been such a powerful reminder for me when fear tries to hold me back.

Peikwen Cheng Thank you for listening to my wild ideas and then helping open the doors to making my ideas a reality. This book would not have been possible without your advice in everything from photography to navigating Chinese culture. And many thanks to your entire family for helping weave the web of possibility and opportunities while we lived our chapter in China. Their support is immeasurable.

Juling He Thank you for your patience and hard work while we explored China on the rails, in the kitchens, eating in restaurants, and navigating the intricacies of Chinese Internet. I truly appreciated your strength and support through the ups and downs of this journey.

Bee Yinn Low Thank you for encouraging me in this project by inspiring me to blog my stories and recipes, with hopes for a book in the future. You are one of my mentors and I'm grateful for your guidance.

Elaine and Yung-chi Cheng Thank you both for your support and love as Peikwen and I followed our passions while living in China. Thank you for reading my blogs in both English and Chinese and commenting along the way. Thank you also for connecting me to wonderful families who contributed to this book. There's so much more to be grateful for to you both. This is just a start.

Gao Jia Thank you for helping me create the first processes in my project and for your patience along the road.

Jordan Wittrock Thank you for accompanying me during the first series of family visits and for your open mind and helpfulness. And thank you for helping me with testing recipes. I am so grateful that we as family have this adventure to share in our memories.

Tranh Pham Thank you for being a team player during our family visits in Jiangsu, Nanjing, and Shanghai. Thanks for keeping the budget and for your constant support. I am also grateful that our friendship will have these memories to look back upon.

MeiLi Coon They say in China "Everything is possible, but everything is difficult." Thank you for keeping the light of possibility turned on while we followed our hearts and realized our passions, sometimes in the shadows of uncertainty.

Chozie You are the amazing connector and ever-energetic spirit behind my journey in China. Thank you for the introductions, the events, and for being part of my China family.

Margherita Liu Thank you for every lesson and coaching session in Mandarin. Your Mandarin lessons at Mandarin Zone School Beijing made my conversations at family meals possible and enjoyable.

Shauna Cho Thank you for the great restaurant opening experience, for the market trips, and for recipe testing while we featured some of the dishes at Paper. And thanks to your father and mother for allowing us the space to launch our dreamy ideas.

Chen Yang Thank you for hosting a Show-Shanti workshop in noodle making at Yellow River Noodles. I miss *biang biang mian* like you can't even imagine.

Lillian Chou Thank you for your guidance as I learned to review restaurants in Beijing. And thank you for sharing your knowledge about food as we reviewed restaurants together.

Paul Kohler Thank you for helping me on the weekends by entertaining Miles while I wrote this book. Also, thank you for being my enthusiastic and honest taste-tester. I'm sure now you can attest to the healthiness of my Chinese recipes. Thank you for your support and your words of encouragement as I nervously started writing this book. I love you.

Thank you to each family listed below for welcoming me into your homes and your kitchens, and sharing your family recipes. Not only have you helped me discover real Chinese food, but now through this book and ShowShanti.com, you have all helped people all around the world realize that Chinese food is more than sweet and sour pork.

Chen Weihua 陈伟华, Gong Donghua 龚冬华, and Chen Chen 陈晨 (Shanghai)

Chen You Gui 陈友贵, Liu Ming Fen 刘明芬, and Chen Jian 陈建 (Suijiang, Yunnan)

Chen Zhigang 陈志刚, Chen Qiufan 陈秋凡, Chen Lu 陈潞 (Foshan, Guangdong)

Fang Runhua 方润花, Gong Xiumei 弓秀梅, Feng Runmei 冯润梅, Qiao Le 乔乐, Qiao Fang 乔芳, Qiao Dan 乔丹, Qiao Xiaoyan 乔小燕 (Jining, Inner-Mongolia)

Gao Songbo 高松波, Han Xianming 韩先明, and Gao Jia 高佳 (Tongzhou, Beijing)

Han Fei (Fifi) 韩菲, Shi Hui Min 师慧敏, Quan Hui Ying 全慧英, Han Bin Quan 韩斌全 (Shanghai)

Jiang Yi 蒋毅 and Jiang Li 蒋利 (Chengdu, Sichuan)

Li Yunzhou 李运洲 and Zhou Yi 周熠 (Changde, Hunan)

Li Min 李敏 and Zhu Lequan 朱乐全 (Kunshan, Jiangsu)

Li Qiang 李强, Zhang Lijuan 张丽娟, and Li Jianhui 李建辉 (Wuding, Yunnan)

Li Shilong 李仕龙, Yang Yilan 杨益兰, and Li Hao 李浩 (Lijiang, Yunnan)

Liu Mingqian 刘明谦, Wu Rong 吴蓉, and Liu Lu 刘璐 (Suijiang, Yunnan)

Liu Ping 刘平, Guo Hui 郭会, and Liu Qianyun 刘倩云 (Pingshan, Sichuan)

Luo Zhen 罗震, Xiao Xia 肖霞, Luo Xiao 罗霄, and Luo Shijia 罗世家 (Chengdu, Sichuan)

Ma Hong Xian 马洪贤 (Puji Zhen, Zhangqiu, Shandong)

Ma Pei, Ma Hong Yu 马洪玉, Zhang Wen Xin 张文新 (Zhangqiu, Shandong)

Shi Qiang 师强, Zhou Juxiang 周菊香, and Shi Yao Xiao Le 师尧小乐 (Changsha, Hunan)

Sun Juan 孙娟, Lu Guangrong 路广荣, and Mao Weiwei 毛薇薇 (Nanjing, Jiangsu)

Xu Weiwen 许伟文, Li Ping 李萍, and Xu Lijia 许利嘉 (Wuxi, Jiangsu)

Yang Ailian 杨爱连, Xie Yang 谢阳, Li Ping 李平, and Xie Jiaying 谢佳颖 (Changde, Hunan)

Yang Hongying 杨宏影 and Wang Shuling 王淑玲 (Chengdu, Sichuan)

Yang Baichen 杨白琛, Wu Fuji 武馥骥, and Wu Songwen 吴松文 (Kunming, Yunnan)

Yang Xukun 杨旭昆, Liu Mingqin 刘明琴, and Yang Yating 杨雅婷 (Kunming, Yunnan)

Zhang Yong 张勇, Wang Bing 王冰, and Zhang Yuqing 张宇晴 (Tongzhou, Beijing)

Zhang Bowei 张伯伟, Ou Youping 区友萍, Zhang Xiaoqiang 张小强, and Zhang Xiaoen 张小恩 (Gaoming, Guangdong)

Zhang Lin 张林, Yang Yang 杨阳, and Zhang Lidan 张力丹 (Suijiang, Yunnan)

Zhang Zhiying 张志英, Gu Qianxing 顾乾行, Sun Lianzhen 孙连珍, Zhang Xiulan 张秀兰, Sun Jianyu 孙建玉, Gu Jing 顾静, and Sun Jiongxian 孙炅贤 (Wuxi, Jiangsu)

Zhang Xinyu 张欣雨, Zhong Yanjin 钟衍津, and Zhang Shixuan 张仕宣 (Chengdu, Sichuan)

Zhong Manqiu 钟曼秋, Li Jian 黎坚, and Li Disha 黎狄莎 (Yulin, Guangxi)

Zhou Qilin 周奇林, father, Luo Aihua 罗爱华, Zhou Ting 周婷, Zhou Jie 周杰, Luo Jianhua 罗建华, Tao Jingsong 陶静松, Zhou Qìngshēng 周庆生, and Luo Zhengwen 罗政文 (Changsha, Hunan)

Many thanks to my taste-testers and supporters throughout my journey of learning how to cook Chinese food: Alethea Lam, Kerena Lam, Shane Christensen, Virginia Christensen, Tranh Pham, Tim Spross, Bill Cheng, Claire Boyd, Cristina McLauchlan, Lin Lin, Kristine Eng, Cynthia & Andrew Browne, Angela May, Shinmin Li, Mix Shell, Veronica Chou, Yang Yating, Wes Chen, Philana Woo, Kalyanee Mam, Darah and Marshall Rosyln, Heather and Ian Aaker, Stacey and Derek Mitchell, April and Justin Knapp, Katharina and Christian Humbert, Jack and Jennifer Orsulak, Joanna Riley, Jennifer Thomé, Jeff Gao, Kristina Leipold, Christina Aman Riglet, Enoch Li, Lisa Qin, Lindsey Roon Wiedmann, Gwo Lee and Mark Dreyer, Candice Yu, and Sheng Nian Yang. My apologies to anyone I've missed in my acknowledgments. I may have forgotten to add you but know that I am sincerely grateful.

RESOURCES

Amazon.com General online retailer. Some stores that carry Chinese ingredients are: CNsnack, Lee Kum Kee, and Spicely Organics.

Asian markets These grocers focus on products used in Asian cuisine. They may also be able to special-order items and answer questions about products or substitutions.

CUESA.org Center for Urban Education about Sustainable Agriculture. San Francisco-based nonprofit focusing on sustainability.

Eleanorhoh.com "Wokstar" website offering a variety of resources, including products (such as a starter kit including an already-seasoned wok), techniques, classes, and healthy eating tips.

Hmart.com Asian supermarket chain.

Local farmers' markets An excellent resource for information on fresh produce and meats. Many follow strict ethical and sustainable practices similar to those of organic purveyors.

Localharvest.org Guide to farms, CSAs, farmers' markets, farm stands, and U-pick produce.

Ranch 99 (99ranch.com) Asian supermarket chain and online retailer carrying imported specialty foods plus meat, seafood, produce, and baked goods.

Showshanti.com Online resource I created containing more recipes, stories, and tips on cooking Chinese.

Whole Foods (Wholefoodsmarket.com) Supermarket chain.

Wokshop.com/newstore San Francisco store and online retailer selling woks and cooking accessories.

RECIPE INDEX

INDEX

CPSIA information can be obtained
at www.ICGtesting.com
Printed in the USA
BVOW05s1434151116

467921BV00001B/1/P

9 781623 157616